How to become an IAM Architect: Expert level

James Relington

DEDICATION

This book is dedicated to all the professionals working tirelessly to secure digital systems and protect organizations from ever-evolving threats. To the cybersecurity teams, IT administrators, and identity management experts who ensure safe and seamless access for users— your work is invaluable. And to my family and friends, whose support and encouragement made this journey possible, thank you.

AKNOWLEDGEMENTS

I would like to express my deepest gratitude to everyone who contributed to the creation of this book. To my colleagues and mentors in the cybersecurity field, your insights and expertise have been invaluable. To the organizations and professionals who shared their experiences and best practices, your contributions have enriched this work. A special thank you to my family and friends for their unwavering support and encouragement throughout this journey. Finally, to the readers, thank you for your interest in identity lifecycle management—may this book help you navigate the evolving landscape of digital security with confidence.

Designing Scalable IAM Architectures for Global Enterprises

Designing a scalable Identity and Access Management (IAM) architecture for global enterprises is a complex challenge that requires careful planning, robust technology selection, and alignment with business and regulatory requirements. Organizations operating across multiple regions, cloud environments, and on-premises systems must ensure that their IAM infrastructure can handle millions of identities while maintaining security, availability, and performance. Scalability in IAM is not just about supporting more users but also about handling high authentication and authorization requests, integrating diverse identity sources, and enforcing dynamic access policies across multiple platforms and geographies.

A fundamental aspect of scalability in IAM is choosing the right architecture. Traditional monolithic IAM solutions struggle to scale effectively under the demands of global enterprises. Instead, modern IAM architectures favor a distributed, microservices-based model that allows individual components—such as authentication, authorization, user provisioning, and auditing—to scale independently. Implementing IAM services as containerized workloads in cloud-native environments enables enterprises to dynamically allocate resources based on demand, ensuring seamless user experiences even during peak usage. Serverless IAM components, such as authentication APIs running on AWS Lambda or Azure Functions, further enhance scalability by automatically handling traffic spikes without requiring manual intervention.

Identity federation is another critical element in scaling IAM architectures. Large organizations often operate in complex IT environments with multiple directories, SaaS applications, and cloud providers. Rather than managing multiple IAM silos, enterprises should implement a federated identity model using standards like Security Assertion Markup Language (SAML), OpenID Connect

(OIDC), and OAuth2. By leveraging identity federation, organizations can authenticate users once and grant access across multiple systems without requiring separate credentials for each application. Global enterprises should also implement Just-in-Time (JIT) provisioning to dynamically create user accounts in target applications upon successful authentication, reducing administrative overhead and ensuring that access is granted only when needed.

The scalability of an IAM system also depends on the performance of authentication and authorization workflows. Traditional authentication mechanisms, such as username-password combinations, introduce bottlenecks due to password resets, account lockouts, and credential stuffing attacks. To enhance performance and scalability, enterprises should implement passwordless authentication methods such as FIDO2, WebAuthn, and biometric authentication. Additionally, Single Sign-On (SSO) solutions reduce the number of authentication events required, improving the user experience and reducing authentication-related infrastructure load.

Authorization mechanisms must also scale efficiently in a global IAM architecture. Traditional Role-Based Access Control (RBAC) models become unmanageable in large organizations due to role explosion, where an excessive number of roles are required to represent different access scenarios. Instead, enterprises should implement Attribute-Based Access Control (ABAC) or Policy-Based Access Control (PBAC) using solutions like Open Policy Agent (OPA) or XACML. These models enable dynamic authorization decisions based on user attributes, environmental factors, and contextual data, allowing organizations to enforce fine-grained access control without excessive administrative overhead.

Global enterprises must also account for regional regulatory requirements when designing scalable IAM architectures. Data residency laws, such as the European Union's General Data Protection Regulation (GDPR) and China's Personal Information Protection Law (PIPL), mandate that user identity data be stored and processed within specific geographic boundaries. IAM architectures must incorporate region-aware identity stores and deploy identity services across multiple data centers to comply with these regulations while maintaining low-latency authentication and authorization for users worldwide. Implementing an edge-based identity strategy, where authentication occurs closer to the user via globally distributed points of presence, helps optimize performance while ensuring compliance.

Resiliency is a critical factor in scalable IAM architectures. High availability must be designed into IAM systems to prevent authentication and authorization outages that could disrupt business operations. Enterprises should deploy IAM services in an active-active configuration across multiple regions, ensuring that authentication requests are automatically routed to the nearest healthy instance in case of failures. Load balancing, caching mechanisms, and database replication strategies further enhance availability by distributing authentication and authorization workloads efficiently. Implementing session replication and token synchronization across IAM nodes ensures seamless user experiences even during failovers.

Scalability also extends to IAM analytics and monitoring. Large-scale IAM deployments generate vast amounts of identity-related events, including login attempts, privilege escalations, and access revocations. To detect anomalies and security threats, enterprises must implement real-time identity analytics using SIEM solutions such as Splunk, ELK, or Azure Sentinel. Machine learning-based anomaly detection further enhances security by identifying unusual access patterns that may indicate credential compromise or insider threats. Scalable IAM architectures must also include centralized logging and audit capabilities to meet compliance requirements and facilitate forensic investigations when security incidents occur.

Another essential consideration in scalable IAM architectures is automation. Manually managing identity lifecycles for thousands or millions of users is not feasible in large enterprises. IAM solutions must integrate with automated identity provisioning and deprovisioning systems using standards like System for Cross-domain Identity Management (SCIM) and APIs for seamless identity synchronization across applications. Enterprises should also adopt Infrastructure-as-Code (IaC) approaches, using tools like Terraform, Ansible, and Kubernetes Operators to automate IAM service deployment and configuration. Automated policy enforcement, such as dynamic privilege escalation and revocation based on risk signals, further enhances scalability and security.

The rise of multi-cloud environments adds another layer of complexity to IAM scalability. Enterprises using AWS, Azure, and Google Cloud simultaneously must ensure that IAM policies, identity synchronization, and access control are consistently applied across all cloud providers. Implementing a centralized identity provider (IdP) with cloud-agnostic IAM policies enables organizations to maintain a unified access control model while leveraging the best capabilities of each cloud provider. Additionally, multi-cloud IAM architectures should support workload identity federation, enabling applications and services to authenticate securely across cloud environments without hardcoded credentials.

As global enterprises continue to expand, their IAM architectures must evolve to support emerging business requirements, new regulatory landscapes, and growing security threats. Designing for scalability from the outset ensures that IAM systems remain resilient, efficient, and secure, regardless of the number of identities they manage. By embracing cloud-native technologies, automation, identity federation, and advanced authorization models, enterprises can build IAM architectures that not only scale but also provide a seamless and secure user experience across diverse environments.

Zero Trust IAM: Architecting Perimeterless Security Models

Zero Trust Identity and Access Management (IAM) represents a paradigm shift in enterprise security, moving away from traditional perimeter-based defenses to a model where trust is never assumed, and every request must be verified dynamically. As organizations embrace cloud computing, remote work, and highly distributed environments, the conventional security model—where users inside the corporate network are implicitly trusted—has become obsolete. Instead, Zero Trust IAM requires continuous authentication, least privilege access, and real-time risk assessment to protect enterprise assets from both external threats and insider risks. Architecting a perimeterless security model with Zero Trust IAM demands a fundamental rethinking of identity management, authentication workflows, and authorization mechanisms.

At the core of Zero Trust IAM is the principle of "never trust, always verify." Unlike legacy IAM models that authenticate users once and grant broad access based on network location or predefined roles, Zero Trust IAM continuously validates identities and enforces strict access controls based on contextual signals. Authentication in a Zero Trust environment must be adaptive, leveraging multiple factors such as device health, user behavior, geolocation, and real-time threat intelligence. This approach ensures that access is granted only when all risk signals indicate a legitimate request, reducing the attack surface and minimizing the impact of credential compromise.

Identity is the foundation of a Zero Trust architecture. Every user, device, application, and service must have a verifiable identity, authenticated and authorized dynamically before gaining access to resources. Strong authentication mechanisms such as passwordless authentication, FIDO2-based biometrics, and public key infrastructure (PKI) enhance security while reducing reliance on traditional passwords, which remain one of the weakest links in enterprise security. Multi-Factor Authentication (MFA) is a fundamental requirement, but in a Zero Trust model, MFA must be adaptive, enforcing additional verification steps based on the sensitivity of the resource being accessed and the perceived risk level of the request.

Authorization in a Zero Trust IAM model must move beyond traditional Role-Based Access Control (RBAC), which often grants excessive permissions and leads to privilege creep. Instead, enterprises should implement Attribute-Based Access Control (ABAC) or Policy-Based Access Control (PBAC) to enforce fine-grained, context-aware access decisions. Policies should be dynamically evaluated using real-time telemetry from identity providers, endpoint security solutions, and threat intelligence platforms. For example, a user accessing a sensitive financial application from an unmanaged device outside corporate premises might be required to perform additional verification steps or be restricted to read-only access.

Least privilege access is a fundamental principle of Zero Trust IAM. Users and services should only be granted the minimum permissions necessary to perform their tasks, and these permissions should be dynamically adjusted based on risk signals. Just-In-Time (JIT) access provisioning further reduces the attack surface by granting temporary privileges only when required, automatically revoking access once the task is completed. Privileged Access Management (PAM) solutions play a critical role in Zero Trust architectures by enforcing strict controls over administrative access, continuously monitoring privileged sessions, and requiring step-up authentication for high-risk operations.

In a perimeterless security model, network-based trust is eliminated, requiring strong authentication and authorization controls at every layer of access. Traditional VPN-based access controls are no longer sufficient, as they provide overly broad access once a user is authenticated. Instead, enterprises should implement identity-aware proxies and secure access service edge (SASE) architectures to enforce identity-driven access controls at the application layer. These solutions allow organizations to provide secure, granular access to resources without exposing entire networks, reducing the risk of lateral movement in the event of credential compromise.

Device identity and health are critical factors in Zero Trust IAM. Authenticating a user without verifying the security posture of their device introduces significant risk, as compromised endpoints can serve as entry points for attackers. Zero Trust IAM architectures must integrate with endpoint detection and response (EDR) solutions to continuously assess device health and enforce access policies accordingly. A user attempting to access corporate resources from a device infected with malware or lacking the latest security updates may be denied access or required to complete additional verification steps.

Visibility and continuous monitoring are essential components of Zero Trust IAM. Enterprises must collect and analyze authentication logs, access events, and behavioral analytics in real time to detect anomalous activity and enforce risk-based access decisions. Security Information and Event Management (SIEM) platforms, User and Entity Behavior Analytics (UEBA), and artificial intelligence-driven threat detection solutions enhance visibility by identifying suspicious patterns, such as unusual login locations, impossible travel scenarios, and abnormal privilege escalations. These insights enable automated responses, such as blocking access, requiring re-authentication, or alerting security teams to potential threats.

Zero Trust IAM also extends to workloads and machine identities. As enterprises move towards cloud-native architectures, securing human identities alone is insufficient. Applications, APIs, microservices, and containers must also adhere to Zero Trust principles, requiring authentication and authorization before communicating with other services. Identity-centric security solutions such as SPIFFE (Secure Production Identity Framework for Everyone) and Istio service mesh enable mutual TLS (mTLS)-based authentication and enforce fine-grained access policies across distributed microservices. Implementing workload identity federation further strengthens security by allowing cloud-native applications to authenticate securely without relying on static credentials.

The shift to Zero Trust IAM requires organizations to adopt a holistic approach to security, integrating IAM with broader cybersecurity initiatives. Enterprises must break down silos between identity management, endpoint security, network security, and threat intelligence to create a unified Zero Trust framework. Automating identity governance and access controls through policy-driven workflows reduces administrative burden while ensuring compliance with security policies. Additionally, organizations must embrace a culture of continuous security validation, conducting regular penetration testing, red teaming exercises, and adversary simulation to identify weaknesses in their Zero Trust IAM implementations.

Transitioning to a Zero Trust IAM model is not a one-time project but an ongoing journey. Organizations must continuously refine their access control policies, update authentication mechanisms, and adapt to evolving threat landscapes. As attackers develop more sophisticated techniques to bypass traditional security controls, enterprises must remain proactive, leveraging AI-driven security analytics, risk-based authentication, and adaptive access controls to stay ahead of emerging threats. By architecting a perimeterless security model based on Zero Trust IAM principles, organizations can enhance security resilience, reduce the risk of identity-based attacks, and ensure that access to critical resources is granted based on verified trust rather than assumed privilege.

IAM Reference Architectures: Enterprise, Multi-Cloud, and Hybrid Models

Identity and Access Management (IAM) is the cornerstone of modern enterprise security, providing mechanisms for authentication, authorization, and governance across a vast array of applications, systems, and cloud environments. As organizations expand their digital footprint, IAM architectures must evolve to support complex enterprise IT landscapes that span on-premises data centers, multi-cloud environments, and hybrid infrastructures. Designing scalable, secure, and resilient IAM reference architectures is essential to ensuring seamless access control, regulatory compliance, and operational efficiency. Enterprises must select the right IAM models based on their business needs, security requirements, and the level of integration required across diverse platforms.

Traditional enterprise IAM architectures were built for centralized control within corporate networks, relying on on-premises identity providers, directory services, and authentication gateways. These models were designed for environments where users, applications, and data primarily resided within the enterprise perimeter. Active Directory (AD) and Lightweight Directory Access Protocol (LDAP)-based IAM systems formed the backbone of identity management, providing centralized authentication, role-based access control (RBAC), and user provisioning. However, as organizations adopted cloud services, these legacy IAM models struggled to extend beyond corporate firewalls, leading to challenges in managing identities across disparate environments.

Enterprise IAM architectures today require a federated approach to identity management, where a central identity provider (IdP) authenticates users and issues tokens that allow seamless access to multiple applications. Security Assertion Markup Language (SAML), OpenID Connect (OIDC), and OAuth2 are the foundational protocols for identity federation, enabling enterprises to integrate with third-party SaaS applications, cloud platforms, and external business partners. Federation reduces identity silos, simplifies access control, and enhances security by allowing organizations to enforce consistent authentication policies across multiple systems. By implementing Just-In-Time (JIT) provisioning, enterprises can dynamically create user accounts in cloud applications, ensuring that access is granted only when required.

Multi-cloud IAM architectures introduce additional complexity, as enterprises leverage multiple cloud providers such as AWS, Azure, and Google Cloud to run critical workloads. Each cloud provider offers its own IAM framework, such as AWS IAM, Azure Active Directory (Azure AD), and Google Cloud IAM, making it challenging to enforce consistent access policies across platforms. A well-designed multi-cloud IAM architecture integrates these native IAM solutions into a unified identity fabric, enabling centralized policy enforcement and identity synchronization. Organizations should adopt a cloud-agnostic IAM approach by implementing a centralized IdP that supports multi-cloud authentication and authorization, reducing the need for managing separate identity silos across cloud environments.

In a multi-cloud IAM model, workload identity management is as crucial as user authentication. Cloud-native applications, APIs, and microservices require secure, scalable authentication mechanisms that do not rely on static credentials. Enterprises should implement service-to-service authentication using federated identities, OAuth2 client credentials, and workload identity federation. Security mechanisms such as SPIFFE (Secure Production Identity Framework for Everyone) and Istio-based service mesh enable mutual TLS (mTLS)-based authentication, ensuring that microservices can securely communicate across different cloud environments without hardcoded credentials.

Hybrid IAM architectures are necessary for organizations that maintain both on-premises systems and cloud-based applications. A hybrid IAM model enables seamless identity management across legacy enterprise systems and modern cloud services, ensuring users have a consistent authentication experience regardless of where an application resides. One of the biggest challenges in hybrid IAM is synchronizing identities between on-premises directory services, such as Active Directory, and cloud-based IdPs. Enterprises must implement identity synchronization tools, such as Azure AD Connect or third-party solutions, to ensure that user attributes, group memberships, and access policies remain consistent across environments.

Hybrid IAM architectures should also incorporate conditional access policies that enforce dynamic authentication requirements based on user location, device health, and risk signals. By integrating with endpoint security solutions and security information and event management (SIEM) platforms, IAM systems can assess risk in real-time and adapt authentication flows accordingly. For example, a user attempting to access a sensitive financial application from an unmanaged device outside corporate premises may be required to complete additional multi-factor authentication (MFA) steps before gaining access.

Regulatory compliance is a critical consideration in IAM reference architectures. Enterprises operating in multiple jurisdictions must ensure their IAM implementations align with data protection laws such as the General Data Protection Regulation (GDPR), the California Consumer Privacy Act (CCPA), and industry-specific regulations such as HIPAA and PCI-DSS. Data sovereignty requirements mandate that user identity data be stored and processed within specific geographic regions, requiring IAM architectures to support region-aware identity stores and access policies. Organizations must implement access governance frameworks that provide continuous monitoring, audit trails, and role-based access reviews to meet compliance obligations.

IAM architectures must also support modern authentication paradigms such as passwordless authentication, biometric authentication, and adaptive authentication. Passwords remain one of the weakest links in security, and enterprises should transition to passwordless solutions using FIDO2, WebAuthn, and public key infrastructure (PKI). Adaptive authentication mechanisms leverage machine learning and behavioral analytics to assess risk signals and dynamically adjust authentication requirements based on user behavior.

Scalability is another key challenge in IAM reference architectures, as enterprises must handle millions of authentication and authorization requests daily. To ensure high availability and performance, IAM components should be deployed in an active-active configuration across multiple regions, with load balancing and database replication strategies in place. Implementing distributed session management using JSON Web Tokens (JWTs), OAuth2 token introspection, and scalable token caching solutions such as Redis and Memcached improves authentication performance while reducing latency.

Enterprises must also consider IAM automation as part of their architecture strategy. Manual identity provisioning and access reviews are time-consuming and error-prone, making automation essential for scalability and security. IAM automation can be achieved through policy-driven workflows, self-service access request portals, and Infrastructure-as-Code (IaC) approaches using Terraform, Ansible, and Kubernetes Operators. By integrating IAM with security orchestration, automation, and response (SOAR) platforms, enterprises can enforce real-time access revocation in response to security incidents, reducing the risk of unauthorized access.

As enterprise IT environments continue to evolve, IAM reference architectures must be designed with flexibility, security, and scalability in mind. Whether managing identities across traditional enterprise applications, multi-cloud infrastructures, or hybrid deployments, organizations must adopt a strategic IAM approach that integrates modern authentication mechanisms, centralized policy enforcement, and real-time security intelligence. By implementing robust IAM architectures, enterprises can provide secure, seamless access to resources while maintaining compliance and protecting against identity-based threats.

Cross-Domain IAM Federation Strategies for Mergers & Acquisitions

Identity and Access Management (IAM) plays a critical role in mergers and acquisitions (M&A), where integrating disparate IT environments, user identities, and access policies is essential for business continuity, security, and regulatory compliance. During an M&A process, organizations must bridge multiple identity domains, each with its own directory services, authentication protocols, and security policies.

Cross-domain IAM federation enables seamless interoperability between different identity systems, allowing users from one organization to securely access resources in the other without requiring separate credentials. Implementing a well-architected federation strategy ensures that business operations remain uninterrupted while minimizing security risks and administrative overhead.

One of the primary challenges in IAM integration during M&A is the coexistence of multiple identity providers (IdPs) and directory services. Organizations undergoing a merger often rely on different IAM platforms, such as Microsoft Active Directory (AD), Azure AD, Okta, Ping Identity, or custom-built identity solutions. Directly merging these identity systems can be complex, time-consuming, and fraught with security risks. Instead of rushing into full directory consolidation, enterprises should first establish federated trust relationships between the existing identity domains. Federation allows users from one company to authenticate using their existing credentials while gaining secure access to resources in the newly acquired organization.

Federation relies on industry-standard protocols such as Security Assertion Markup Language (SAML), OpenID Connect (OIDC), and OAuth2 to enable cross-domain authentication and authorization. By leveraging these standards, organizations can establish trust between identity providers without requiring extensive modifications to existing IAM infrastructures. A common approach is to configure a primary identity provider that acts as a central authentication hub, aggregating authentication requests from multiple federated domains. This enables users to log in once and access applications across both organizations, reducing friction and improving the user experience.

Single Sign-On (SSO) is a key component of federated IAM strategies in M&A scenarios. SSO allows employees from both organizations to authenticate once and gain access to all authorized applications without repeated logins. Implementing SSO across federated domains improves productivity by eliminating the need for users to manage multiple sets of credentials. Additionally, it enhances security by reducing password fatigue and lowering the risk of credential reuse or phishing attacks. Organizations should deploy SSO solutions that support multi-protocol federation, ensuring seamless integration regardless of the identity providers in use.

Just-in-Time (JIT) provisioning further simplifies IAM federation by dynamically creating user accounts in the target organization's applications upon successful authentication. Rather than manually provisioning accounts for thousands of newly acquired employees, JIT provisioning automatically syncs user attributes from the source identity provider, ensuring that access is granted in real-time. This approach reduces administrative overhead and accelerates the onboarding process while maintaining security controls through predefined attribute mappings and access policies.

IAM federation strategies must also address role and permission mapping between organizations. Each company in an M&A scenario may have its own role-based access control (RBAC) model, with different role definitions, access groups, and privilege levels. Directly mapping these roles between organizations can be challenging, as role structures often vary significantly. A more flexible approach is to implement attribute-based access control (ABAC), where access decisions are based on user attributes such as job function, department, and security clearance rather than predefined roles. This allows for dynamic access control policies that can be adjusted as organizational structures evolve post-merger.

Security and compliance are major concerns when integrating IAM systems across merged entities. Organizations must ensure that federated authentication adheres to security best practices, including Multi-Factor Authentication (MFA), risk-based authentication, and conditional access policies. MFA should be enforced consistently across federated domains to prevent unauthorized access, especially for privileged accounts and high-risk transactions. Risk-based authentication leverages contextual signals such as device health, IP reputation, and geolocation to dynamically adjust authentication requirements, mitigating potential threats from compromised accounts.

Regulatory compliance adds another layer of complexity to cross-domain IAM federation in M&A scenarios. Organizations operating in multiple jurisdictions must ensure that identity data transfers comply with data protection regulations such as the General Data Protection Regulation (GDPR), the California Consumer Privacy Act (CCPA), and industry-specific frameworks like HIPAA and PCI-DSS. Data residency requirements may necessitate localized identity stores or region-specific access controls. IAM federation architectures must be designed to enforce granular data access policies while ensuring compliance with regulatory mandates.

IAM federation in M&A also requires robust identity lifecycle management to handle user onboarding, role transitions, and deprovisioning. When organizations merge, employees may change roles, move between business units, or leave the company entirely. Without proper IAM governance, orphaned accounts and excessive privileges can introduce security vulnerabilities. Automated identity governance solutions help streamline user lifecycle management by ensuring that access rights are provisioned, modified, and revoked in accordance with organizational policies. Regular access reviews and audits further strengthen security by identifying and mitigating unnecessary or excessive privileges.

Hybrid and multi-cloud environments further complicate cross-domain IAM federation in M&A scenarios. Organizations that operate across AWS, Azure, and Google Cloud must ensure that IAM federation extends seamlessly across cloud platforms while maintaining consistent access policies. Cloud-native IAM solutions such as AWS IAM Identity Center, Azure AD B2B, and Google Cloud IAM support federated authentication, enabling cross-cloud identity integration. Organizations should adopt a cloud-agnostic identity federation strategy that unifies authentication and authorization across multiple cloud providers while avoiding vendor lock-in.

As IAM federation is established post-merger, organizations should also implement continuous monitoring and anomaly detection to identify potential security threats. Federated authentication logs should be integrated with Security Information and Event Management (SIEM) solutions to provide real-time visibility into authentication patterns, failed login attempts, and unusual access behaviors. User and Entity Behavior Analytics (UEBA) further enhances security by detecting anomalous identity activity, such as credential sharing or privilege escalation attempts. Automated response mechanisms, such as adaptive authentication and access revocation, help mitigate threats before they escalate.

Cultural and organizational alignment is another crucial aspect of IAM federation in M&A. Employees from different companies may be accustomed to different authentication workflows, access request processes, and security policies. A well-planned IAM integration strategy must include user training, change management, and clear communication to ensure a smooth transition. Providing self-service access portals, unified authentication experiences, and responsive IT support enhances user adoption and minimizes disruption during the merger process.

Successfully implementing IAM federation strategies for M&A requires a balance between security, usability, and operational efficiency. By leveraging federated authentication protocols, automating identity lifecycle management, enforcing consistent security policies, and ensuring regulatory compliance, organizations can streamline the integration of IAM systems while reducing risk. The ability to establish seamless identity federation across multiple domains accelerates business integration, enhances security resilience, and enables organizations to fully realize the strategic value of their mergers and acquisitions.

Architecting Decentralized Identity Solutions with SSI and Blockchain

Decentralized identity represents a fundamental shift in how identities are managed, authenticated, and verified across digital ecosystems. Traditional identity systems rely on centralized identity providers, such as governments, enterprises, and social platforms, to issue and validate credentials. However, these centralized models present several challenges, including privacy concerns, data breaches, identity fraud, and user dependency on third-party institutions. Self-Sovereign Identity (SSI), enabled by blockchain technology, offers an alternative approach where individuals and entities gain full control over their digital identities, eliminating reliance on intermediaries while ensuring security, privacy, and interoperability.

In a decentralized identity architecture, identities are no longer stored in a single directory or controlled by a central authority. Instead, users generate and manage their own cryptographic identity keys, which they use to request, store, and present digital credentials from multiple issuers. These credentials, known as verifiable credentials (VCs), can be shared with service providers as proof of identity without exposing unnecessary personal data. The underlying blockchain serves as a trust anchor, enabling cryptographic verification of credentials without relying on a centralized identity provider. This architecture aligns with the principles of privacy by design, where users disclose only the minimum information necessary for a given transaction.

A core component of SSI is decentralized identifiers (DIDs), which are unique, blockchain-anchored identity references that replace traditional usernames and email-based identifiers. Unlike centralized identity models where identifiers are managed by identity providers, DIDs are owned and controlled by users, allowing them to create multiple identity representations for different contexts without linking them to a single entity. DIDs are resolvable through a decentralized ledger, where cryptographic proofs validate the authenticity of identity claims without requiring direct communication with the issuing authority. This mechanism ensures that identity verification remains tamper-proof and independent of any single organization.

The decentralized identity trust model consists of three primary actors: issuers, holders, and verifiers. Issuers, such as governments, universities, and enterprises, create and sign verifiable credentials that attest to specific attributes of an identity. Holders, typically individuals or organizations, store these credentials in secure digital wallets and present them selectively based on contextual requirements. Verifiers, such as businesses or online services, validate these credentials using decentralized ledgers to confirm their authenticity without needing to contact the issuer. This model enhances privacy and security by eliminating the need for centralized identity lookups while providing strong cryptographic assurances of identity legitimacy.

Blockchain plays a critical role in decentralized identity architectures by providing an immutable, distributed ledger for anchoring identity-related transactions. Unlike traditional IAM systems that rely on centralized databases prone to breaches, blockchain-based identity solutions distribute trust across multiple nodes, reducing single points of failure and enhancing resilience. Public, permissioned, and hybrid blockchain models can be used depending on privacy, scalability, and governance requirements. Public blockchains, such as Ethereum and Bitcoin, offer high transparency and decentralization but may introduce scalability challenges. Permissioned blockchains, such as Hyperledger Fabric, provide greater control over access and transaction validation, making them suitable for enterprise identity use cases.

One of the key advantages of decentralized identity solutions is their ability to reduce identity fraud and credential misuse. Traditional identity verification relies on static data points, such as social security numbers and email addresses, which can be easily stolen or forged. In contrast, SSI ensures that credentials are cryptographically signed and stored in user-controlled wallets, making them tamper-proof and resistant to impersonation attacks. Additionally, Zero-Knowledge Proofs (ZKPs) enable users to prove specific attributes, such as age or citizenship, without revealing the actual data, enhancing privacy while maintaining compliance with regulatory requirements.

Interoperability is another crucial factor in decentralized identity architectures. Organizations adopting SSI must ensure that their identity systems are compatible with industry standards, such as the W3C Verifiable Credentials (VC) standard, the Decentralized Identity Foundation (DIF) specifications, and the Trust Over IP (ToIP) framework. Standardized identity schemas and cryptographic protocols facilitate cross-platform identity verification, enabling seamless authentication across different service providers, industries, and jurisdictions. Without interoperability, SSI implementations risk becoming isolated silos, undermining the fundamental goal of decentralization.

Despite its advantages, decentralized identity solutions also present challenges that organizations must address when architecting an SSI-based IAM model. One of the primary concerns is usability. End users must manage their own private keys and digital wallets, which introduces complexities in key recovery, secure storage, and user experience design. Traditional IAM systems handle account recovery through centralized mechanisms, such as email verification or security questions, but SSI eliminates these intermediaries, making key loss a critical risk. To mitigate this, organizations must develop secure key management strategies, such as multi-party computation (MPC), social recovery mechanisms, and threshold cryptography.

Scalability is another challenge when implementing blockchain-based IAM solutions. Public blockchains, while decentralized and secure, face limitations in transaction throughput, latency, and storage efficiency. Organizations deploying SSI architectures must carefully choose blockchain networks that balance decentralization with performance. Layer-2 scaling solutions, such as rollups and sidechains, can improve efficiency by reducing the number of on-chain transactions while maintaining verifiability. Alternatively, hybrid architectures that combine off-chain verifiable credential exchanges with on-chain trust anchors can optimize performance without sacrificing security.

Regulatory compliance remains a significant consideration in decentralized IAM architectures. Many data protection laws, such as GDPR and CCPA, impose strict requirements on data processing, consent management, and user rights over personal information. While SSI enhances privacy by minimizing data exposure, blockchain's immutability can conflict with the right to be forgotten and data rectification requirements. Organizations must design compliance-aware identity solutions that incorporate off-chain storage, revocation mechanisms, and privacy-preserving techniques to align with legal frameworks. Additionally, governance models must be established to define roles, responsibilities, and dispute resolution processes in decentralized identity ecosystems.

Enterprise adoption of decentralized identity requires a strategic transition from traditional IAM models to a more distributed, user-centric approach. Organizations must first assess their identity management needs, existing regulatory obligations, and integration points before deploying SSI solutions. Hybrid models, where decentralized identities coexist with existing IAM frameworks, offer a pragmatic approach to gradual adoption. Enterprises can begin by implementing verifiable credentials for specific use cases, such as workforce identity verification, customer onboarding, and supply chain authentication, before expanding to full SSI integration.

Decentralized identity architectures powered by SSI and blockchain have the potential to redefine digital identity management by empowering users with control, enhancing security, and reducing reliance on centralized authorities. As enterprises, governments, and industry consortiums collaborate to develop scalable, interoperable SSI frameworks, decentralized identity solutions will become a cornerstone of the next-generation IAM landscape, enabling secure and privacy-preserving authentication in a hyper-connected world.

IAM Governance Frameworks: Defining Policies, Standards, and Best Practices

Identity and Access Management (IAM) governance is a fundamental aspect of enterprise security and compliance, ensuring that access to systems, applications, and data is managed in a structured, consistent, and secure manner. As organizations grow and adopt cloud, hybrid, and multi-cloud environments, IAM governance frameworks become critical for defining policies, enforcing access controls, and maintaining regulatory compliance. Without a well-defined governance model, enterprises risk security breaches, regulatory penalties, and operational inefficiencies resulting from mismanaged identities and excessive access privileges. A strong IAM governance framework establishes the foundational policies, standards, and best practices necessary to manage identities effectively across complex IT ecosystems.

IAM governance begins with a clear definition of policies that outline how identities are created, managed, and revoked within an organization. These policies should specify identity lifecycle management processes, including user provisioning, access requests, role assignments, and deprovisioning. Identity lifecycle governance ensures that users receive appropriate access based on their job functions while minimizing the risk of privilege creep, where users accumulate excessive permissions over time. Organizations must enforce policies that automatically adjust user access as employees change roles, move between departments, or leave the company. Automating identity lifecycle processes reduces administrative overhead and improves security by ensuring that orphaned accounts and unnecessary access privileges are promptly removed.

Access control policies form a critical component of IAM governance frameworks. Organizations must define role-based access control (RBAC), attribute-based access control (ABAC), or policy-based access control (PBAC) models to regulate user permissions. RBAC structures access based on predefined roles, making it easier to assign permissions to groups of users. However, RBAC can become complex and difficult to manage as enterprises scale, leading to role explosion. ABAC offers a more dynamic approach by granting access based on attributes such as job function, location, and risk factors. PBAC further enhances access control by evaluating policies dynamically, leveraging real-time context to determine access eligibility. IAM governance frameworks should establish standardized models for access control enforcement while maintaining flexibility for evolving business needs.

A crucial aspect of IAM governance is the implementation of least privilege principles. Users should only be granted the minimum level of access required to perform their job responsibilities. Organizations must enforce least privilege access through fine-grained permissions, privilege escalation workflows, and periodic access reviews. Implementing Just-in-Time (JIT) access provisioning enhances security by granting temporary elevated privileges only when necessary and revoking them automatically once the task is completed. This reduces the risk of insider threats and limits the potential impact of compromised accounts.

Multi-Factor Authentication (MFA) policies are essential for securing IAM environments, particularly for privileged users and high-risk access scenarios. IAM governance frameworks must mandate MFA requirements based on risk assessment, ensuring that authentication methods align with industry best practices. Adaptive authentication further strengthens security by dynamically adjusting authentication requirements based on factors such as user behavior, device health, and login patterns. By enforcing risk-based authentication policies, organizations can reduce friction for low-risk transactions while applying stronger controls to sensitive operations.

IAM governance frameworks must also address regulatory compliance requirements. Organizations operating across different industries and jurisdictions must align their IAM policies with compliance frameworks such as GDPR, HIPAA, SOX, PCI-DSS, and ISO 27001. Regulatory compliance mandates stringent access controls, audit logging, and identity verification mechanisms to protect sensitive data. Enterprises must establish governance policies that enforce access certification reviews, ensuring that users maintain appropriate permissions in accordance with compliance standards. Automating compliance reporting and audit trail generation reduces the burden on security teams and ensures that IAM processes remain transparent and auditable.

Access request and approval workflows play a vital role in IAM governance, ensuring that users obtain the necessary permissions without exposing systems to unauthorized access. Organizations should implement self-service access request portals integrated with automated approval workflows based on predefined policies. Role-based approval hierarchies streamline the access request process while maintaining security controls. For high-risk permissions, governance frameworks should enforce additional approval steps, such as managerial review, risk assessment, or security team validation. By implementing well-defined access request workflows, organizations enhance efficiency while maintaining control over privilege escalations.

IAM governance frameworks must include robust identity verification mechanisms to prevent fraudulent account creation and unauthorized access. Identity proofing techniques, such as document verification, biometric authentication, and federated identity validation, enhance the security of user onboarding processes. Organizations should enforce identity verification policies tailored to risk levels, ensuring that high-privilege accounts undergo stricter identity validation. By integrating identity proofing solutions with IAM workflows, enterprises mitigate the risk of identity fraud and account takeovers.

Privileged Access Management (PAM) is a critical component of IAM governance, addressing the security challenges associated with administrative and high-privilege accounts. PAM policies should enforce session monitoring, password vaulting, and just-in-time privilege elevation to minimize the risk of privilege abuse. IAM governance frameworks must establish PAM access control models that limit administrative access based on time, task, and risk analysis. Continuous monitoring of privileged activities, coupled with anomaly detection, enhances security visibility and reduces the risk of unauthorized privilege escalation.

IAM governance frameworks should also incorporate identity analytics and anomaly detection to enhance threat mitigation capabilities. By leveraging machine learning and behavioral analytics, organizations can identify suspicious identity activities such as unauthorized login attempts, privilege misuse, and insider threats. Security Information and Event Management (SIEM) solutions and User and Entity Behavior Analytics (UEBA) platforms play a crucial role in IAM governance by providing real-time identity threat intelligence. Implementing automated response mechanisms, such as risk-based access revocation and session termination, strengthens security while minimizing manual intervention.

IAM governance must extend to third-party and vendor identity management, ensuring that external users and contractors adhere to the same security standards as internal employees. Governance policies should define strict access controls for third-party accounts, enforce least privilege principles, and require periodic access recertification. Organizations should implement federated identity management models that enable secure authentication for external users without granting direct access to internal IAM systems. By applying strong governance controls to third-party identities, organizations mitigate supply chain risks and prevent unauthorized access.

Continuous improvement and policy refinement are essential for effective IAM governance. Organizations must regularly review and update their IAM policies, incorporating lessons learned from security incidents, audit findings, and evolving business requirements. Governance frameworks should establish IAM steering committees responsible for defining policies, assessing risks, and ensuring alignment with organizational security objectives. Regular IAM maturity assessments help organizations identify gaps, optimize access control models, and enhance overall identity security posture.

A well-architected IAM governance framework provides the foundation for secure and compliant identity management. By defining clear policies, enforcing least privilege access, implementing adaptive authentication, and leveraging identity analytics, organizations can establish robust governance controls that protect against identity-related threats while ensuring seamless and efficient access for users. As enterprises adopt cloud-native and decentralized identity models, IAM governance must evolve to address new security challenges while maintaining regulatory compliance and operational effectiveness.

Advanced Trust Models in Federated IAM: Multi-Hop and Transitive Trust

Federated Identity and Access Management (IAM) enables organizations to establish trust relationships between different identity providers (IdPs) and service providers (SPs), allowing users to authenticate once and gain access to multiple systems without needing separate credentials. While traditional federation models rely on direct trust between two entities, advanced IAM architectures require more sophisticated trust mechanisms to support multi-hop authentication and transitive trust relationships. These models are essential for large enterprises, multi-cloud environments, government-to-business collaborations, and cross-border federations where direct trust is impractical or infeasible. Implementing multi-hop and transitive trust models in federated IAM requires a deep understanding of trust propagation, security risks, and policy enforcement mechanisms.

In a standard federated IAM model, an identity provider directly issues authentication assertions to a service provider based on an established trust relationship. This one-to-one trust model works well in simple scenarios but becomes limiting when users need access across multiple domains that do not share direct trust. Multi-hop trust extends federation by allowing an intermediary IdP to relay authentication assertions between different entities. In this model, a user authenticates with their home IdP, which then issues an assertion that is consumed by an intermediary IdP before being passed along to the final SP. This chaining of identity assertions allows organizations to connect disparate identity domains without requiring every SP to establish trust with every IdP individually.

Multi-hop trust models are commonly used in large-scale federations such as national identity frameworks, intergovernmental organizations, and multinational enterprises that operate across different regulatory jurisdictions. For example, in a cross-border digital identity system, a national IdP may not directly trust all foreign service providers but can trust a regional identity broker that facilitates authentication requests. When a user attempts to access a foreign SP, the authentication request flows through the national IdP to the identity broker, which then forwards the assertion to the target SP. This approach simplifies identity federation by reducing the number of direct trust relationships while maintaining interoperability between different identity ecosystems.

Transitive trust extends the concept of multi-hop authentication by allowing trust to propagate beyond the initial federation participants. In a transitive trust model, if entity A trusts entity B and entity B trusts entity C, then entity A implicitly trusts entity C. This model is particularly useful in large federations where establishing direct trust relationships with every participant would be impractical. However, transitive trust introduces significant security and governance challenges, as an organization may inadvertently trust entities that it has never explicitly vetted. Without proper trust constraints, transitive trust can lead to unintended access permissions, increasing the risk of security breaches.

To mitigate the risks associated with transitive trust, organizations must implement strict trust policies and enforce constraints on trust propagation. One common approach is to use trust metadata, which defines the allowed trust paths and enforces restrictions on authentication assertion forwarding. Trust frameworks such as the InCommon Federation in higher education and the eduGAIN network for global research institutions use metadata registries to define trusted IdPs and SPs, preventing unauthorized trust relationships from forming. By carefully curating these trust registries, organizations can limit transitive trust exposure while maintaining the benefits of federated authentication.

Another critical aspect of managing multi-hop and transitive trust is assertion integrity and validation. When an authentication assertion passes through multiple intermediaries, there is an increased risk of assertion modification, replay attacks, and unauthorized attribute injection. To prevent these risks, federated IAM architectures must enforce strong cryptographic controls, including digital signatures and assertion expiration mechanisms. Each intermediary IdP in a multi-hop authentication flow must verify the integrity of incoming assertions before forwarding them to the next entity. Additionally, organizations should enforce attribute validation policies to ensure that only authorized identity attributes are relayed to downstream SPs.

Policy-based trust evaluation is essential in transitive trust models to ensure that access decisions align with security and compliance requirements. Instead of blindly accepting authentication assertions from any trusted intermediary, SPs should evaluate trust conditions dynamically based on predefined policies. Policy engines such as Open Policy Agent (OPA) and XACML-based access control frameworks enable organizations to define granular trust policies that assess factors such as assertion issuer reputation, authentication context strength, and real-time risk signals. These policies can dynamically determine whether to accept, reject, or require additional verification for transitive trust assertions.

Federated IAM frameworks must also address identity governance challenges in multi-hop and transitive trust environments. As trust relationships scale across multiple domains, organizations need visibility into authentication flows, identity assertions, and access patterns. Centralized logging and auditing of federated transactions provide critical insights into trust propagation, enabling security teams to detect anomalies and enforce compliance requirements. Security Information and Event Management (SIEM) solutions and identity analytics platforms play a key role in monitoring federated IAM ecosystems, helping organizations identify potential trust abuses or misconfigurations.

One of the major use cases for multi-hop and transitive trust models is in cloud service federation. Enterprises adopting multi-cloud strategies often integrate with multiple cloud identity providers such as AWS IAM, Azure AD, and Google Cloud IAM. Rather than managing separate authentication integrations for each cloud provider, organizations can establish a central identity hub that federates authentication requests to multiple cloud platforms. In this model, employees authenticate with the corporate IdP, which then federates authentication to the respective cloud IdP based on predefined trust rules. This approach simplifies cloud IAM management while ensuring secure and consistent access policies across different providers.

Multi-hop and transitive trust are also critical for secure business-to-business (B2B) and government-to-business (G2B) identity federations. Large enterprises often collaborate with multiple partners, suppliers, and contractors, each with its own identity management system. Instead of requiring direct trust relationships with every partner, organizations can use identity brokers or federated identity hubs to facilitate secure authentication flows. This model allows external partners to authenticate using their corporate credentials while enforcing centralized trust policies that restrict access based on risk, contract terms, or compliance requirements.

The implementation of advanced trust models in federated IAM requires continuous assessment and governance. Organizations must periodically review trust relationships, revoke obsolete trust links, and update trust policies based on evolving business requirements and security threats. Automated trust lifecycle management solutions can streamline this process by detecting unauthorized trust changes, enforcing periodic trust re-evaluations, and providing real-time insights into trust dynamics.

By leveraging multi-hop and transitive trust models, organizations can build scalable, interoperable IAM ecosystems that support complex identity federation requirements. However, the success of these models depends on strong governance controls, cryptographic safeguards, and dynamic policy enforcement mechanisms. As federated IAM architectures continue to evolve, organizations must remain vigilant in managing trust relationships, ensuring that authentication assertions remain secure, verifiable, and aligned with enterprise security objectives.

Architecting IAM for Large-Scale Cloud-Native Applications

Identity and Access Management (IAM) is a foundational component of cloud-native architectures, enabling secure authentication, authorization, and governance across distributed systems. As enterprises transition to cloud-native application development, traditional IAM models struggle to scale efficiently in highly dynamic environments. Large-scale cloud-native applications operate across multiple cloud providers, microservices, containers, and serverless workloads, requiring a robust and flexible IAM architecture that can handle millions of identities, real-time access control decisions, and high-velocity authentication requests. Designing an IAM framework for cloud-native applications demands a shift from monolithic identity management approaches to decentralized, API-driven, and policy-based access models that support elasticity, resilience, and zero-trust security principles.

Authentication in cloud-native applications must accommodate diverse identity sources, including enterprise directories, social identity providers, external partners, and machine identities. Centralized identity providers (IdPs) such as Azure Active Directory (Azure AD), AWS IAM Identity Center, and Google Cloud IAM offer federated authentication capabilities using industry standards such as OpenID Connect (OIDC), Security Assertion Markup Language (SAML), and OAuth2. For large-scale deployments, organizations must implement federated authentication models that enable seamless access across multi-cloud environments while maintaining centralized identity governance. Decoupling authentication from application logic ensures that identity validation is handled by dedicated IdPs, improving security and scalability.

Microservices-based applications introduce additional complexity in IAM design, as each service must authenticate users, enforce fine-grained authorization policies, and securely communicate with other services. Traditional session-based authentication models are ineffective in cloud-native architectures due to their reliance on centralized session stores, which create bottlenecks and fail to scale efficiently. Instead, large-scale applications should leverage stateless authentication mechanisms such as JSON Web Tokens (JWTs) or OAuth2 access tokens, which allow authentication information to be securely embedded within tokens and verified without requiring database lookups. Token-based authentication enables services to scale independently and reduces the need for persistent session storage, improving performance and resilience.

Authorization in cloud-native IAM architectures must be dynamic and context-aware. Static role-based access control (RBAC) models are inadequate for large-scale applications due to role explosion and lack of real-time decision-making. Attribute-based access control (ABAC) and policy-based access control (PBAC) offer more scalable alternatives by allowing access decisions to be based on user attributes, environmental context, and real-time risk signals. Implementing a centralized policy engine, such as Open Policy Agent (OPA) or XACML-based authorization frameworks, enables dynamic policy evaluation while keeping access control logic decoupled from application code. Fine-grained authorization models ensure that cloud-native applications enforce least privilege access at every layer, reducing the risk of over-permissioned identities.

Identity federation across multiple cloud providers is a critical requirement for large-scale cloud-native applications. Enterprises often operate in multi-cloud environments where workloads are distributed across AWS, Azure, and Google Cloud, each with its own IAM framework. Implementing workload identity federation allows applications and services running in different cloud environments to authenticate securely without relying on long-lived credentials or static API keys. Using workload identity federation mechanisms such as AWS IAM Roles for Service Accounts (IRSA), Google Workload Identity Federation, and Azure Managed Identities enables secure cross-cloud authentication while enforcing identity governance policies centrally.

Service-to-service authentication is a key consideration in cloud-native IAM architectures. Microservices and APIs must authenticate and authorize each other securely without exposing credentials or hardcoded secrets. Implementing mutual TLS (mTLS) authentication using service mesh technologies like Istio or Linkerd provides strong identity assurance for inter-service communication. Service mesh-based IAM integrates workload identities into the underlying network fabric, enabling encrypted communication and automated certificate management. Additionally, using OAuth2 client credentials flow for API authentication ensures that only authorized services can invoke protected endpoints, reducing the risk of unauthorized access.

Privileged Access Management (PAM) must also be extended to cloud-native environments to prevent credential misuse and insider threats. Traditional PAM solutions were designed for static IT environments, but cloud-native applications require ephemeral credential management that aligns with DevOps and Infrastructure-as-Code (IaC) practices. Implementing just-in-time (JIT) privilege escalation for cloud resources, ephemeral credentials for administrative access, and automated secret rotation using tools like HashiCorp Vault, AWS Secrets Manager, and Azure Key Vault enhances security while minimizing standing privileges. Cloud-native PAM solutions integrate with IAM policies to enforce temporary access based on risk and business justification.

Scalability is a defining characteristic of IAM in cloud-native architectures. Large-scale applications must support millions of authentication and authorization requests per second, requiring distributed and horizontally scalable IAM components. Implementing rate limiting, token caching, and edge-based authentication helps reduce latency and improve system performance. By leveraging content delivery networks (CDNs) and identity-aware proxies, authentication workloads can be offloaded to distributed edge locations, improving response times while reducing backend processing overhead.

Event-driven identity automation is another crucial aspect of IAM for cloud-native applications. Traditional IAM systems rely on periodic access reviews and batch-based provisioning, which cannot keep pace with the dynamic nature of cloud-native workloads. Implementing real-time identity event processing using Kafka, AWS EventBridge, or Google Pub/Sub allows IAM systems to respond instantly to identity changes, risk signals, and policy violations. Automating identity lifecycle events, such as provisioning, role assignments, and revocations, ensures that access remains aligned with security policies and compliance requirements.

Compliance and auditability remain critical considerations in cloud-native IAM architectures. Large-scale applications must maintain visibility into authentication events, access decisions, and identity-related activities across multi-cloud environments. Centralized logging using OpenTelemetry, Fluentd, or ELK Stack enables organizations to collect and analyze IAM events in real time, supporting compliance reporting and security investigations. Integrating IAM logs with SIEM platforms and User and Entity Behavior Analytics (UEBA) enhances threat detection by identifying anomalies such as credential misuse, privilege escalation, and suspicious access patterns.

IAM governance in cloud-native applications must extend beyond human identities to include non-human entities such as service accounts, IoT devices, and AI-based workloads. Managing machine identities at scale requires automated certificate issuance, workload identity federation, and policy-driven identity governance frameworks. Implementing lifecycle management for machine identities ensures that non-human accounts do not retain excessive privileges beyond their intended purpose, reducing security risks in large-scale deployments.

As enterprises continue adopting cloud-native architectures, IAM must evolve to meet the demands of scale, security, and agility. Designing a cloud-native IAM framework requires a combination of decentralized authentication, fine-grained authorization, workload identity federation, and real-time identity automation. By implementing scalable, API-driven IAM models that align with DevOps and Zero Trust principles, organizations can secure large-scale applications while enabling seamless access across distributed environments.

Resilient IAM Architectures: Designing for Failover, HA, and DR

Identity and Access Management (IAM) is a mission-critical component of enterprise security and IT infrastructure. If IAM services become unavailable, users and applications lose access to essential systems, disrupting business operations and exposing organizations to security risks. To mitigate these risks, enterprises must design resilient IAM architectures that ensure high availability (HA), failover capabilities, and disaster recovery (DR) strategies. A well-architected IAM system must not only support continuous authentication and authorization but also recover rapidly from failures without compromising security or performance.

High availability (HA) is the foundation of resilient IAM architectures, ensuring that authentication, authorization, and identity governance services remain operational even during infrastructure failures. Achieving HA in IAM requires a distributed architecture with redundant components deployed across multiple regions and availability zones. By implementing active-active or active-passive clustering models, organizations can prevent single points of failure and ensure seamless failover in case of service disruptions. Active-active configurations provide load-balanced traffic distribution across multiple IAM nodes, improving both resilience and performance. Active-passive architectures, on the other hand, maintain standby replicas that take over operations only when the primary system fails.

Load balancing plays a crucial role in HA for IAM. Large-scale IAM deployments rely on traffic distribution mechanisms to ensure that authentication requests are handled efficiently across multiple servers. Global load balancers, such as AWS Elastic Load Balancing (ELB), Azure Front Door, and Google Cloud Load Balancing, direct requests to the healthiest IAM instances based on availability and proximity. Local load balancers within data centers further optimize IAM traffic distribution, preventing any single server from being overwhelmed by authentication and authorization requests. Integrating auto-scaling mechanisms ensures that IAM services can dynamically adjust to changing workloads, maintaining performance during peak demand periods.

Failover mechanisms are essential to IAM resilience, ensuring that authentication services remain available even when primary nodes become unreachable. Automated failover strategies leverage health checks and monitoring tools to detect service failures and redirect requests to backup IAM instances. Organizations should implement DNS failover techniques to reroute authentication traffic to alternative endpoints when primary services experience downtime. Using IAM service discovery frameworks, such as HashiCorp Consul or Kubernetes-based service mesh solutions, enables dynamic failover routing based on real-time system health.

Database replication is a critical factor in IAM failover design. IAM services rely heavily on identity directories, policy stores, and session databases to process authentication and authorization requests. Enterprises must ensure that IAM databases are replicated across multiple locations to prevent data loss and improve redundancy. Multi-master replication models allow read and write operations to occur simultaneously across multiple database instances, ensuring continuous availability. Read replicas can offload query workloads, improving IAM system performance while maintaining fault tolerance. Database failover automation using managed solutions such as AWS RDS Multi-AZ, Azure SQL Geo-Replication, and Google Cloud Spanner further enhances IAM resilience.

Disaster recovery (DR) strategies are essential for IAM architectures to recover from large-scale failures, including data center outages, cyberattacks, and natural disasters. A comprehensive DR plan for IAM includes geographically distributed backup sites, automated backup replication, and well-defined recovery time objectives (RTOs) and recovery point objectives (RPOs). IAM backup and restoration procedures must be regularly tested to ensure data integrity and service continuity. Organizations should implement IAM backup encryption to protect sensitive identity data from unauthorized access during storage and transit.

IAM systems must also support cross-region failover to ensure resilience against regional outages. Multi-region IAM architectures leverage cloud-native IAM services, such as AWS IAM, Azure AD, and Google Cloud IAM, to replicate authentication and authorization policies across different geographies. By synchronizing IAM policies, access logs, and user identities across multiple regions, enterprises can maintain consistent access control even when a primary region becomes unavailable. Federated IAM models further enhance cross-region resilience by enabling identity federation between separate IAM domains, ensuring users can authenticate via alternative pathways.

Session management resilience is another key consideration in IAM high availability design. When IAM services experience downtime, active user sessions should remain valid to prevent session disruptions. Stateless authentication using JSON Web Tokens (JWTs) allows session information to be validated independently of the IAM database, reducing dependency on real-time database lookups. Token revocation lists and OAuth2 introspection endpoints provide mechanisms to manage session expiration and mitigate risks associated with long-lived access tokens.

IAM architectures must also integrate with logging and monitoring solutions to detect failures and security threats in real time. Centralized IAM logging using OpenTelemetry, Fluentd, or the ELK stack enables organizations to track authentication events, authorization decisions, and access anomalies across distributed IAM environments. Security Information and Event Management (SIEM) solutions help correlate IAM logs with security incidents, enabling proactive threat detection and automated response actions. IAM monitoring dashboards should provide real-time visibility into authentication latencies, failed login attempts, and directory replication health, ensuring that administrators can quickly address issues before they escalate into system-wide failures.

Automation plays a crucial role in IAM resilience by enabling self-healing mechanisms that restore services without manual intervention. Infrastructure-as-Code (IaC) tools, such as Terraform, AWS CloudFormation, and Azure Resource Manager, allow IAM infrastructure to be automatically redeployed in response to failures. Kubernetes-based IAM deployments benefit from automated container restarts, scaling, and rolling updates to ensure continuous availability. Implementing IAM orchestration frameworks that integrate with incident response workflows ensures that recovery actions are triggered based on predefined SLAs and security policies.

IAM resilience must also extend to hybrid and multi-cloud environments. Enterprises that operate across multiple cloud providers and on-premises infrastructures must ensure that IAM services remain operational regardless of where authentication requests originate. Hybrid IAM architectures leverage cloud-based IAM solutions, such as Okta, Ping Identity, and ForgeRock, to provide identity redundancy while maintaining integration with legacy directory services. Multi-cloud IAM strategies employ identity federation and workload identity management to synchronize access control policies across AWS, Azure, and Google Cloud, ensuring that authentication services remain consistent across diverse environments.

Testing and validation are critical components of IAM resilience planning. Organizations should conduct regular failover drills, disaster recovery simulations, and IAM penetration tests to validate their HA and DR strategies. Red teaming exercises that simulate IAM service failures and adversarial attacks help identify weaknesses in failover mechanisms and refine incident response playbooks. Automated IAM resilience testing frameworks can continuously validate authentication workflows, access controls, and policy enforcement under failure scenarios, ensuring that IAM systems remain robust and adaptive.

By designing IAM architectures with high availability, failover automation, and disaster recovery planning, enterprises can ensure that identity services remain resilient against disruptions, security threats, and large-scale outages. A well-architected IAM resilience strategy not only enhances system reliability but also strengthens enterprise security by maintaining continuous identity verification and access control enforcement.

Designing IAM Architectures for Critical Infrastructure and ICS/OT Security

Identity and Access Management (IAM) for critical infrastructure and Industrial Control Systems (ICS) and Operational Technology (OT) security presents unique challenges compared to traditional IT environments. Unlike enterprise IT systems, where IAM is primarily designed for employees, cloud applications, and APIs, IAM in ICS/OT environments must account for a diverse range of users, devices, and systems, including human operators, automated control systems, sensors, and remote maintenance teams. These environments operate under strict uptime requirements, often running 24/7, where any disruption to authentication or authorization mechanisms can impact safety, production, and national security. A well-architected IAM framework for ICS/OT must balance security, availability, and operational efficiency while mitigating evolving cyber threats targeting critical infrastructure.

Traditional IAM models do not easily apply to ICS/OT environments due to their reliance on legacy systems, air-gapped networks, and proprietary protocols. Many industrial environments were designed decades ago without security-by-design principles, meaning they lack modern identity management capabilities such as federated authentication, role-based access control (RBAC), and centralized identity governance. Retrofitting IAM into these environments requires careful consideration of compatibility, latency constraints, and regulatory requirements. Identity integration strategies must accommodate both legacy and modernized ICS assets without introducing disruptions or excessive administrative overhead.

Authentication in ICS/OT environments must support diverse identity sources, including local operator credentials, hardware-based authentication, and federated identities for remote access. Password-based authentication is often inadequate due to shared operator terminals, lack of robust credential management, and susceptibility to phishing and brute-force attacks. Instead, organizations should implement strong authentication mechanisms such as Multi-Factor Authentication (MFA), Public Key Infrastructure (PKI), and biometric authentication. Hardware-based authentication using smart cards, cryptographic tokens, and TPM (Trusted Platform Module) integrations enhances security while reducing the reliance on static passwords.

One of the critical challenges in ICS/OT IAM is managing remote access securely. Industrial environments often require remote support from third-party vendors, engineers, and maintenance teams who need temporary access to critical systems. Implementing Zero Trust-based IAM models ensures that no remote user or device is implicitly trusted. Strong identity verification, Just-in-Time (JIT) access provisioning, and continuous session monitoring should be enforced for remote access. Identity-aware proxies, virtual jump boxes, and privileged session monitoring solutions provide additional layers of security by ensuring that remote users are authenticated and monitored in real-time.

Authorization in ICS/OT IAM must be highly granular to prevent excessive privileges and unauthorized actions that could disrupt industrial processes. Role-based access control (RBAC) remains a foundational approach, but static role definitions can lead to over-provisioning of privileges. Instead, Attribute-Based Access Control (ABAC) and Policy-Based Access Control (PBAC) provide more dynamic authorization models based on real-time context, such as operator location, device status, and operational risk level. Implementing fine-grained authorization policies ensures that only authorized personnel can modify system configurations, issue control commands, or access sensitive data.

Machine identity management is a critical component of IAM for ICS/OT security. Unlike traditional enterprise environments, where identities are primarily human users, ICS/OT networks rely heavily on machine-to-machine (M2M) communication. Industrial sensors, controllers, SCADA (Supervisory Control and Data Acquisition) systems, and IIoT (Industrial Internet of Things) devices must authenticate and securely communicate with each other. Using certificate-based authentication, mutual TLS (mTLS), and workload identity federation ensures that only trusted machines can interact within the ICS environment. Automated certificate lifecycle management prevents expired or misconfigured certificates from causing disruptions in automated processes.

IAM architectures for ICS/OT must support air-gapped and isolated environments where cloud-based identity services may not be feasible. Many critical infrastructure sectors, such as energy, transportation, and manufacturing, operate in highly controlled network segments that restrict external connectivity. IAM solutions must be designed to function offline while ensuring periodic synchronization with central identity repositories. Implementing lightweight directory services, such as read-only Active Directory replicas or local LDAP servers, allows for local authentication while maintaining centralized identity governance. Offline authentication mechanisms, such as hardware-based tokens and biometric authentication, further enhance security in disconnected environments.

Logging and auditing are essential for IAM governance in ICS/OT environments. Every authentication event, authorization request, and privilege escalation should be logged and monitored to detect anomalies and potential security incidents. Unlike traditional IT environments, where log aggregation is centralized in SIEM (Security Information and Event Management) platforms, ICS/OT logging must account for operational constraints such as bandwidth limitations and real-time processing requirements. Implementing distributed logging architectures with edge-based log collection and real-time event correlation ensures visibility without impacting system performance. Advanced User and Entity Behavior Analytics (UEBA) further enhances security by identifying anomalous operator activities, insider threats, and compromised accounts.

Compliance with regulatory frameworks is a key driver for IAM in ICS/OT environments. Industrial sectors are subject to stringent cybersecurity regulations, such as the NERC CIP (North American Electric Reliability Corporation Critical Infrastructure Protection), IEC 62443 (Industrial Automation and Control Systems Security), and the EU NIS Directive (Network and Information Security Directive). IAM architectures must enforce compliance-driven access control policies, periodic access reviews, and strict identity verification processes. Automated compliance reporting and real-time access audits help organizations demonstrate adherence to regulatory requirements while reducing administrative burdens.

Resilience and failover mechanisms must be built into ICS/OT IAM architectures to ensure continuous availability of authentication and authorization services. Downtime in IAM systems can disrupt industrial operations, leading to production losses, safety risks, and regulatory non-compliance. Implementing high-availability IAM clusters, geo-redundant identity stores, and automated failover mechanisms ensures that IAM services remain operational even during infrastructure failures. Identity replication across multiple data centers, redundant authentication pathways, and local failover identity providers enhance the resilience of IAM in critical environments.

Supply chain security is another critical aspect of IAM for ICS/OT. Industrial organizations rely on third-party vendors for system maintenance, software updates, and equipment monitoring, introducing potential security risks. IAM solutions must enforce strict vendor identity verification, time-restricted access policies, and secure remote access gateways to mitigate supply chain threats. Implementing federated identity management for third-party vendors allows for seamless yet controlled access while maintaining strong auditability and compliance oversight.

Architecting IAM for ICS/OT environments requires a combination of traditional IAM best practices and industry-specific security controls. By integrating strong authentication mechanisms, fine-grained authorization policies, machine identity management, regulatory compliance frameworks, and resilient failover mechanisms, organizations can build robust IAM architectures that secure critical infrastructure while ensuring operational continuity. The evolving threat landscape targeting ICS/OT systems underscores the need for proactive IAM strategies that align with Zero Trust principles, risk-based access control, and continuous identity monitoring.

Global Identity Management: Architecting for Regional Compliance and Data Sovereignty

Managing identity at a global scale introduces a complex set of challenges that go beyond authentication and authorization. Organizations operating in multiple countries must navigate diverse regulatory landscapes, data sovereignty requirements, and compliance mandates that dictate how identity data is stored, processed, and accessed. Architecting a global identity management (IAM) framework requires a balance between security, scalability, and adherence to regional legal frameworks. Without a well-defined IAM strategy, enterprises risk non-compliance, data residency violations, and operational inefficiencies. A robust global IAM architecture must support federated authentication, regional data partitioning, and regulatory-driven access control models to meet the evolving needs of global enterprises.

Data sovereignty regulations require organizations to store and process identity-related information within specific geographic regions. Laws such as the European Union's General Data Protection Regulation (GDPR), China's Personal Information Protection Law (PIPL), and Russia's Federal Law on Personal Data dictate strict rules on how identity data must be handled. Non-compliance with these regulations can result in hefty fines, legal penalties, and reputational damage. To address these challenges, global IAM architectures must incorporate regional identity stores that align with data residency laws. Deploying identity services in localized data centers ensures that user credentials, authentication logs, and access policies remain within compliant jurisdictions while maintaining availability and performance for regional users.

Federated identity management is essential for organizations that operate across multiple regulatory environments. Instead of maintaining separate IAM systems for each region, enterprises should implement identity federation models that enable seamless authentication across jurisdictions while ensuring compliance with local laws. Identity federation allows users to authenticate through a central identity provider (IdP) while adhering to regional data protection requirements. Federated authentication using Security Assertion Markup Language (SAML), OpenID Connect (OIDC), and OAuth2 enables organizations to establish trusted identity relationships across different regulatory domains. By leveraging federated authentication, organizations can provide a unified login experience while keeping user identity data localized.

Multi-region IAM architectures must also address cross-border data transfers, which are tightly regulated under various legal frameworks. GDPR imposes strict conditions on transferring personal data outside the European Economic Area (EEA), requiring organizations to implement Standard Contractual Clauses (SCCs) or binding corporate rules (BCRs) to ensure compliance. China's PIPL restricts cross-border data flows and mandates government approval for certain types of data exports. To navigate these regulatory constraints, IAM architectures should implement geo-fencing policies that enforce regional data access restrictions based on user location, data classification, and legal requirements. Geo-fenced IAM policies prevent unauthorized access to identity data from non-compliant regions, reducing the risk of regulatory violations.

Identity governance and administration (IGA) must align with regional compliance mandates to enforce proper access controls, audit logging, and identity lifecycle management. Organizations must establish automated access certification processes that periodically review and validate user entitlements based on jurisdiction-specific policies. Implementing a centralized IGA platform with regional enforcement capabilities allows enterprises to maintain compliance without introducing operational silos. Access governance policies should define role-based access controls (RBAC), attribute-based access controls (ABAC), and least privilege principles based on regional compliance requirements. By enforcing regionalized identity governance models, organizations can mitigate the risk of excessive permissions and unauthorized access.

Authentication mechanisms in global IAM architectures must adapt to regional security policies and regulatory frameworks. Some jurisdictions mandate specific authentication methods, such as biometric authentication, government-issued digital identities, or multi-factor authentication (MFA) protocols. Countries like India promote Aadhaar-based authentication, while the European Union encourages the use of eIDAS-compliant digital identity frameworks. IAM systems must support flexible authentication policies that allow organizations to enforce region-specific authentication requirements while maintaining a consistent global user experience. Adaptive authentication mechanisms, which analyze contextual signals such as device reputation, geolocation, and risk factors, provide dynamic authentication controls tailored to local regulations.

Data minimization is a core principle in global IAM compliance, ensuring that only necessary identity attributes are collected, processed, and stored. Regulatory frameworks such as GDPR and PIPL emphasize strict data retention policies, requiring organizations to delete or anonymize identity data after a predefined period. IAM architectures should incorporate attribute-based identity storage models that allow organizations to store only the essential identity attributes required for authentication and authorization. Implementing dynamic data masking and tokenization techniques further enhances data privacy by restricting sensitive identity information from unauthorized exposure.

Disaster recovery and high availability strategies must be designed to comply with regional data sovereignty requirements. IAM services must operate across multiple regions while ensuring failover mechanisms that do not violate data residency laws. Multi-region IAM replication models should maintain separate identity stores within compliant jurisdictions, preventing unauthorized cross-border replication of sensitive identity data. Implementing failover mechanisms such as active-active IAM clusters, local authentication caches, and regionalized session management ensures that IAM services remain available even during regional outages.

IAM analytics and monitoring in global architectures must align with regional compliance requirements for security event logging and threat detection. Regulatory frameworks such as the U.S. CLOUD Act and China's Cybersecurity Law impose restrictions on how identity logs are stored and accessed. Organizations must implement region-specific log retention policies that prevent unauthorized access to authentication logs from foreign jurisdictions. Deploying distributed security monitoring solutions that operate within regional compliance boundaries ensures that IAM threat intelligence and anomaly detection capabilities remain effective while adhering to local regulations.

Global IAM architectures must also support compliance-driven user consent and preference management. Regulations such as GDPR mandate that users have full control over their identity data, including the ability to review, update, and revoke consent for data processing. IAM platforms must integrate self-service portals that allow users to manage their privacy preferences, control data sharing settings, and request data deletion in compliance with regional laws. Implementing user-centric IAM models that prioritize transparency and user control enhances trust and regulatory alignment.

Supply chain IAM security plays a crucial role in global identity management, ensuring that third-party vendors, contractors, and partners adhere to the same regulatory compliance standards as internal employees. IAM architectures must enforce strict third-party access controls, ensuring that external identities are subject to regional compliance requirements before being granted access to corporate systems. Implementing federated B2B identity management, third-party risk assessments, and vendor access certification processes strengthens IAM governance across global supply chains.

As enterprises expand their global footprint, IAM architectures must evolve to meet the complex regulatory landscape of identity data management. Organizations must implement decentralized identity models, federated authentication mechanisms, and region-specific access policies to balance security, compliance, and operational efficiency. By designing IAM frameworks that accommodate regional data sovereignty requirements while ensuring seamless global authentication, enterprises can achieve compliance, mitigate regulatory risks, and enhance the security posture of their identity infrastructure.

IAM Risk-Based Access Architectures: Adaptive Authentication and AI-Driven Authorization

Identity and Access Management (IAM) has evolved beyond static authentication and authorization models to embrace risk-based access architectures that dynamically adjust access decisions based on real-time security signals. Traditional IAM systems rely on predefined role-based or attribute-based policies, which often grant or deny access without considering contextual risk factors. As cyber threats become more sophisticated, organizations need intelligent IAM architectures that adapt to evolving security risks, user behavior, and environmental conditions. Risk-based access control (RBAC) integrates adaptive authentication and AI-driven authorization to enforce dynamic, context-aware security policies that enhance both security and user experience.

Adaptive authentication is a core component of risk-based IAM architectures, allowing authentication mechanisms to adjust dynamically based on the assessed risk of a given login attempt. Unlike static multi-factor authentication (MFA), which enforces additional verification for all users regardless of risk, adaptive authentication evaluates contextual attributes such as device health, geolocation, network reputation, and historical user behavior before determining the authentication requirements. If a user logs in from a trusted device and location with a consistent behavioral pattern, the system may allow seamless authentication without additional challenges. However, if an anomaly is detected—such as an attempt from an unrecognized device, an unusual geographic location, or a high-risk IP address—the system can enforce step-up authentication, requiring additional factors such as biometrics, FIDO2 authentication, or one-time passcodes (OTPs).

Risk-based authentication (RBA) extends adaptive authentication by continuously assessing risk throughout the user session. Instead of evaluating risk only at login, RBA continuously monitors user activity, detecting potential threats in real-time. For example, if a user logs in from a trusted location but later attempts to access high-privilege applications from an untrusted network, the system can trigger re-authentication or session termination. This continuous risk assessment ensures that authentication remains adaptive to changing conditions, reducing the risk of compromised credentials leading to unauthorized access.

AI-driven authorization enhances traditional access control mechanisms by leveraging machine learning models to make real-time access decisions. Traditional Role-Based Access Control (RBAC) and Attribute-Based Access Control (ABAC) models require predefined rules and policies, which become difficult to manage at scale, leading to excessive privilege accumulation and policy drift. AI-driven authorization dynamically evaluates risk factors such as user behavior anomalies, transaction sensitivity, device telemetry, and external threat intelligence feeds to determine whether access should be granted, denied, or subjected to additional verification.

Machine learning-based behavioral analytics play a crucial role in AI-driven IAM architectures. By analyzing historical access patterns, machine learning models establish baselines for normal user activity and detect deviations that may indicate account compromise or insider threats. For example, if an employee typically accesses enterprise applications from a corporate office during business hours but suddenly attempts access from an unfamiliar geographic location at an unusual time, the system can flag the request as suspicious and enforce additional authentication measures or temporary access restrictions. AI-powered anomaly detection minimizes false positives by continuously refining risk models based on evolving user behaviors.

Risk-based access architectures integrate with User and Entity Behavior Analytics (UEBA) to provide deeper insights into identity-related risks. UEBA solutions analyze authentication logs, access requests, privilege escalations, and transaction behaviors to identify unusual activity patterns. By correlating identity events with broader security intelligence, UEBA enables IAM systems to detect compromised accounts, privilege abuse, and fraudulent access attempts before they escalate into security incidents. Integrating UEBA with AI-driven IAM solutions enhances proactive threat mitigation by enabling automated risk scoring, real-time policy adjustments, and automated remediation actions.

Context-aware access control is another key component of risk-based IAM architectures. Instead of relying solely on static access policies, context-aware authorization evaluates dynamic conditions such as real-time risk scores, environmental attributes, and transaction sensitivity. For example, an employee accessing a financial dashboard from a trusted corporate network may be granted full access, while the same employee attempting access from a public Wi-Fi network may be restricted to read-only permissions or required to complete additional authentication. Context-aware IAM policies enforce the principle of least privilege dynamically, ensuring that access permissions align with real-time risk levels.

Risk-based IAM architectures also integrate with Security Orchestration, Automation, and Response (SOAR) platforms to enable automated identity threat response. When high-risk activity is detected, IAM systems can trigger automated workflows that revoke access, reset credentials, or notify security teams for further investigation. For example, if an IAM system detects an anomalous authentication attempt from a compromised credential database, it can automatically disable the affected user account, trigger an identity verification process, and update access control lists to prevent further exploitation. By integrating IAM with SOAR and SIEM (Security Information and Event Management) solutions, organizations can streamline identity threat detection and response.

Privileged Access Management (PAM) benefits significantly from AI-driven risk-based controls. Traditional PAM solutions enforce static access policies for privileged accounts, but AI-enhanced PAM dynamically adjusts access levels based on risk scores. For example, a privileged user attempting to access critical infrastructure from an unmanaged device may be denied access or required to complete biometric verification. AI-driven PAM also reduces standing privileges by granting just-in-time (JIT) access, where elevated privileges are assigned only for the duration of a task and revoked automatically once the task is completed. This minimizes the attack surface while maintaining operational flexibility.

Risk-based IAM architectures must also consider compliance and regulatory requirements. Many data protection regulations, such as GDPR, CCPA, and PSD2, mandate strong authentication controls and continuous access monitoring. Risk-based authentication and AI-driven authorization help organizations meet compliance mandates by enforcing adaptive access controls that align with regulatory requirements. Implementing continuous risk assessment, automated access reviews, and real-time compliance reporting ensures that IAM systems remain audit-ready and aligned with industry standards.

Scalability is a crucial factor in designing risk-based IAM architectures for large enterprises. Traditional IAM systems struggle to process high volumes of authentication requests and authorization decisions in real time. AI-driven risk engines leverage cloud-based compute power, distributed identity stores, and event-driven architectures to scale IAM operations dynamically. Implementing event-driven identity pipelines using Kafka, AWS EventBridge, or Google Pub/Sub allows organizations to process risk signals asynchronously, reducing latency while maintaining high performance.

Risk-based IAM architectures enhance both security and user experience by minimizing authentication friction for low-risk users while enforcing stricter controls for high-risk scenarios. By integrating adaptive authentication, AI-driven authorization, behavioral analytics, and automated identity threat response, organizations can create intelligent IAM frameworks that dynamically adjust to evolving cyber threats and business requirements. As AI and machine learning continue to evolve, IAM will become increasingly autonomous, enabling enterprises to enforce access policies with greater precision and resilience in the face of emerging identity threats.

Strategic IAM Roadmaps: Aligning IAM with Enterprise Digital Transformation

Identity and Access Management (IAM) is a foundational pillar of enterprise security and business enablement. As organizations embark on digital transformation initiatives, IAM must evolve beyond traditional security functions to become a strategic enabler of agility, innovation, and seamless user experiences. A well-architected IAM roadmap aligns identity management with enterprise goals, ensuring that security policies, access governance, and user identity models support modern digital business strategies. Without a structured IAM strategy, organizations risk fragmented identity systems, inconsistent security policies, compliance gaps, and operational inefficiencies that hinder their transformation journey.

A strategic IAM roadmap begins with a clear understanding of the enterprise's digital transformation objectives. Whether an organization is migrating to cloud platforms, adopting hybrid IT environments, implementing Zero Trust security frameworks, or expanding into new markets, IAM must be designed to support these initiatives. The roadmap should outline how IAM will provide secure access to applications, data, and services across diverse environments while enabling a frictionless user experience. Establishing a long-term vision for IAM ensures that investments in identity technologies align with business growth and evolving security needs.

One of the primary goals of an IAM roadmap is to modernize identity infrastructure to support cloud-first and hybrid IT strategies. Traditional IAM models, which rely on on-premises directory services such as Active Directory and LDAP, struggle to integrate with cloud-native applications and decentralized workforces. Organizations must transition from legacy IAM architectures to cloud-based identity providers (IdPs) that support federated authentication, adaptive access controls, and API-driven integrations. Implementing cloud identity solutions such as Azure AD, AWS IAM Identity Center, or Okta enhances scalability and flexibility while reducing the complexity of managing identities across multiple platforms.

IAM modernization also requires rethinking authentication models to balance security and usability. Password-based authentication has long been a weak link in enterprise security, leading to credential theft, phishing attacks, and password fatigue. A strategic IAM roadmap should prioritize the adoption of passwordless authentication methods, including FIDO2 biometrics, smart cards, and certificate-based authentication. Multi-Factor Authentication (MFA) should be enhanced with adaptive risk-based authentication that dynamically adjusts security controls based on user context, device health, and behavioral analytics. By reducing reliance on static credentials, organizations improve security while delivering a seamless authentication experience for employees, customers, and partners.

Federated identity management is a critical component of IAM roadmaps, enabling seamless authentication across cloud platforms, SaaS applications, and third-party ecosystems. Enterprises that operate across multiple cloud providers, such as AWS, Azure, and Google Cloud, must implement federated IAM models that unify identity governance while maintaining regional compliance. Security Assertion Markup Language (SAML), OpenID Connect (OIDC), and OAuth2 facilitate cross-domain authentication, ensuring that users can access distributed resources without redundant credentials. Federated identity governance also extends to business-to-business (B2B) and business-to-consumer (B2C) interactions, allowing organizations to securely integrate with external partners, suppliers, and customers.

IAM roadmaps must also address the growing need for dynamic authorization frameworks that go beyond static Role-Based Access

Control (RBAC). Traditional RBAC models become increasingly difficult to manage as enterprises scale, leading to role explosion and excessive privilege accumulation. Modern IAM strategies should incorporate Attribute-Based Access Control (ABAC) and Policy-Based Access Control (PBAC), which enable fine-grained, context-aware authorization decisions. Policy engines such as Open Policy Agent (OPA) and XACML-based access control solutions provide real-time authorization enforcement based on user attributes, environmental factors, and risk assessments. By implementing dynamic access policies, organizations ensure that users receive just-in-time permissions based on business context and security posture.

Zero Trust security principles should be integrated into IAM roadmaps to protect against evolving cyber threats. Unlike perimeter-based security models that assume trust within corporate networks, Zero Trust IAM enforces continuous authentication and least privilege access at every interaction. Implementing identity-centric Zero Trust architectures requires continuous identity verification, device posture assessment, and real-time risk analytics. IAM solutions should integrate with endpoint security, security information and event management (SIEM), and behavioral analytics platforms to enforce Zero Trust policies dynamically. By aligning IAM with Zero Trust strategies, organizations reduce the risk of insider threats, compromised credentials, and lateral movement attacks.

Identity governance and administration (IGA) plays a central role in strategic IAM planning, ensuring that user identities, entitlements, and access rights are properly managed throughout their lifecycle. Automated identity lifecycle management simplifies user provisioning, access request approvals, and access certification processes, reducing manual administrative overhead. Identity governance platforms should integrate with HR systems, IT service management (ITSM) tools, and cloud applications to synchronize identity attributes and enforce consistent access policies. Implementing periodic access reviews, risk-based access analytics, and audit trails enhances compliance with regulatory frameworks such as GDPR, HIPAA, and SOX.

IAM analytics and artificial intelligence (AI) provide powerful capabilities for proactive identity threat detection and automated security responses. Machine learning-driven User and Entity Behavior Analytics (UEBA) can detect anomalous access patterns, privilege escalations, and account takeovers by analyzing authentication logs, API access patterns, and user behavior. AI-driven identity risk scoring enables organizations to dynamically adjust authentication and authorization policies in real time. Integrating IAM with Security Orchestration, Automation, and Response (SOAR) platforms further enhances security by enabling automated incident response workflows for identity-related threats.

A strategic IAM roadmap must also include initiatives for workforce IAM, customer IAM (CIAM), and machine identity management. Workforce IAM ensures that employees, contractors, and remote workers have secure access to enterprise resources based on their roles and responsibilities. CIAM focuses on delivering seamless and secure authentication experiences for customers, enabling self-service identity management and consent-driven data sharing. Machine identities, including IoT devices, service accounts, and automated workloads, require robust identity lifecycle management to prevent credential misuse and unauthorized API access. By incorporating workforce, customer, and machine IAM strategies into a unified roadmap, organizations achieve a holistic identity security posture.

IAM transformation requires executive sponsorship, cross-functional collaboration, and continuous improvement. Organizations must establish IAM governance committees that align identity initiatives with enterprise security, compliance, and business objectives. IAM roadmaps should be reviewed periodically to adapt to evolving cybersecurity threats, regulatory changes, and digital business requirements. Investing in IAM training, awareness programs, and change management initiatives ensures that IAM adoption aligns with organizational goals and user expectations.

By aligning IAM with enterprise digital transformation, organizations not only enhance security and compliance but also unlock new business opportunities, improve operational efficiency, and deliver superior user experiences. A strategic IAM roadmap serves as a blueprint for modernizing identity management, enabling secure cloud adoption, supporting Zero Trust architectures, and ensuring that identity security evolves alongside digital business innovation.

Architecting Unified Identity and Access Management Across Cloud Providers

Enterprises increasingly operate in multi-cloud environments, leveraging multiple cloud service providers (CSPs) such as AWS, Microsoft Azure, and Google Cloud Platform (GCP) to meet diverse business and technological needs. While multi-cloud strategies offer flexibility, scalability, and redundancy, they introduce significant challenges for Identity and Access Management (IAM). Each cloud provider has its own native IAM framework, requiring organizations to manage separate identity silos, inconsistent access policies, and complex integration patterns. A unified IAM architecture across cloud providers ensures seamless authentication, consistent authorization policies, and centralized governance, enabling organizations to maintain security and operational efficiency while minimizing identity sprawl.

A fundamental principle of unified IAM across cloud providers is establishing a centralized identity provider (IdP) that serves as the single source of truth for user authentication and access management. By leveraging a federated identity model, enterprises can integrate multiple cloud platforms with a central IdP such as Azure Active Directory (Azure AD), Okta, Ping Identity, or an on-premises identity system with SAML, OpenID Connect (OIDC), or OAuth2 federation capabilities. This approach allows users to authenticate once through the IdP and gain access to resources across different cloud environments without requiring multiple credentials or duplicate accounts. Federated IAM reduces administrative overhead, improves user experience, and strengthens security by enforcing a consistent authentication policy across all cloud services.

Workload identity federation is equally critical in multi-cloud IAM architectures, ensuring that applications, microservices, and automated workloads authenticate securely without reliance on long-lived credentials. Native IAM services such as AWS IAM Roles, Google Workload Identity Federation, and Azure Managed Identities provide secure workload authentication within their respective platforms but do not natively interoperate across cloud boundaries. Implementing a centralized trust model where workloads from different cloud providers authenticate using short-lived, just-in-time credentials or service identity federation enhances security by eliminating hardcoded credentials while enabling seamless cross-cloud authentication. Organizations should adopt federated workload identity frameworks that use token exchange mechanisms to allow applications in one cloud to securely interact with resources in another.

Authorization consistency is a major challenge in unified IAM across cloud providers. Each CSP implements access control differently— AWS relies on IAM policies and roles, Azure uses role-based access control (RBAC) and custom roles, while GCP employs IAM bindings and permissions. These differences make it difficult to enforce consistent least privilege access controls across multi-cloud deployments. Organizations must implement a centralized authorization policy engine, such as Open Policy Agent (OPA) or Cloud Infrastructure Entitlement Management (CIEM) solutions, to define and enforce access policies across all cloud providers. By standardizing access control policies using declarative authorization frameworks, enterprises can ensure that permissions are consistently applied, minimizing privilege sprawl and reducing security risks.

Multi-cloud IAM architectures must also support Just-In-Time (JIT) access provisioning to enforce temporary and least privilege access policies dynamically. Traditional static role assignments can lead to excessive permissions, increasing the attack surface. JIT access provisioning ensures that users, administrators, and workloads receive only the permissions required for a specific task, with automatic expiration upon task completion. This approach significantly reduces standing privileges, mitigating risks associated with credential theft, privilege escalation, and insider threats. Cloud-native access control mechanisms such as AWS IAM Access Analyzer, Google IAM Conditions, and Azure Privileged Identity Management (PIM) should be integrated with JIT workflows to enforce real-time access decisions.

A key component of unified IAM is centralized identity governance and compliance management. Organizations operating in multi-cloud environments must adhere to global regulatory frameworks such as GDPR, HIPAA, PCI-DSS, and CCPA, each imposing strict identity and access control requirements. IAM governance solutions should provide centralized visibility into user access, privileged accounts, and policy violations across all cloud providers. Implementing automated identity lifecycle management, periodic access certification, and real-time policy enforcement ensures continuous compliance while reducing manual effort. Cloud Security Posture Management (CSPM) tools and Identity Threat Detection and Response (ITDR) solutions enhance multi-cloud IAM governance by monitoring access patterns, detecting anomalies, and enforcing security best practices.

Privileged Access Management (PAM) must be extended to multi-cloud environments to secure administrative access to cloud resources. Native cloud IAM mechanisms often lack comprehensive privileged session monitoring, leaving gaps in security controls for high-risk actions. Enterprises should implement cloud-ready PAM solutions that enforce strong authentication, just-in-time privilege escalation, and session recording for privileged cloud activities. By integrating PAM with multi-cloud IAM architectures, organizations ensure that administrative access remains tightly controlled, auditable, and resistant to credential compromise.

Logging, monitoring, and identity analytics play a crucial role in securing multi-cloud IAM architectures. Each cloud provider generates authentication logs, access records, and security events that must be aggregated and analyzed to detect unauthorized access, misconfigured permissions, and identity-based threats. Centralizing IAM logs using OpenTelemetry, Fluentd, or SIEM solutions such as Splunk, Azure Sentinel, or Google Chronicle enhances visibility into authentication trends and access patterns across cloud environments. Machine learning-powered User and Entity Behavior Analytics (UEBA) further strengthens security by detecting anomalous identity activities, such as unusual login attempts, excessive permission changes, or suspicious API calls.

Zero Trust security principles should be embedded in multi-cloud IAM architectures to enforce continuous identity verification and least privilege access. Traditional perimeter-based security models are ineffective in distributed cloud environments, where users, workloads, and data span multiple providers. Zero Trust IAM mandates strong authentication, device security validation, and contextual access controls before granting access to cloud resources. Implementing continuous risk assessment, adaptive authentication, and identity-aware network segmentation ensures that cloud identities remain protected against evolving cyber threats.

Enterprises must also consider automation and Infrastructure-as-Code (IaC) for IAM policy management across cloud providers. Manually configuring IAM policies, roles, and permissions in different cloud environments increases the likelihood of misconfigurations and security gaps. Organizations should use Terraform, AWS CloudFormation, Azure Bicep, and Google Deployment Manager to define IAM policies as code, ensuring consistent and repeatable identity configurations across cloud providers. By embedding IAM policy enforcement into DevSecOps pipelines, security teams can automatically validate identity controls before deploying cloud applications, reducing misconfiguration risks.

As multi-cloud adoption accelerates, organizations must build a unified IAM framework that centralizes authentication, standardizes authorization, and enforces identity governance across all cloud providers. By leveraging federated identity models, workload identity federation, AI-driven access policies, and Zero Trust IAM principles, enterprises can secure their cloud environments while enabling seamless and scalable identity management. A well-architected multi-cloud IAM strategy not only strengthens security but also enhances operational efficiency, reduces complexity, and ensures compliance with global regulatory requirements.

Enterprise Passwordless IAM: Architecting FIDO2 and Biometric Solutions

Password-based authentication has long been the foundation of enterprise Identity and Access Management (IAM), yet it remains one of the weakest links in cybersecurity. Passwords are frequently reused, easily compromised, and susceptible to phishing, brute-force attacks, and credential stuffing. As cyber threats evolve and regulatory requirements mandate stronger authentication measures, enterprises are shifting toward passwordless IAM architectures that enhance security, improve user experience, and reduce the administrative burden associated with password management. Implementing passwordless authentication requires a combination of FIDO2 standards, biometric authentication, hardware security modules (HSMs), and adaptive authentication frameworks to ensure seamless and secure access across enterprise systems.

The foundation of enterprise passwordless IAM is FIDO2, a set of open authentication standards developed by the Fast Identity Online (FIDO) Alliance. FIDO2 consists of the WebAuthn API and the Client to Authenticator Protocol (CTAP), which enable strong, phishing-resistant authentication using cryptographic key pairs stored in secure hardware devices. Unlike traditional authentication methods that rely on shared secrets, FIDO2 authentication is based on asymmetric cryptography, ensuring that private keys never leave the user's device. This eliminates the risk of credential theft, phishing attacks, and password database breaches, making FIDO2 a robust foundation for enterprise passwordless authentication.

WebAuthn, a key component of FIDO2, allows browsers and applications to support passwordless authentication natively. WebAuthn enables users to authenticate using biometrics (such as fingerprints or facial recognition), security keys, or trusted devices without requiring a username and password. Enterprise IAM architectures must integrate WebAuthn with identity providers (IdPs) such as Microsoft Entra ID, Okta, Ping Identity, and ForgeRock to enable seamless passwordless authentication across cloud and on-premises applications. By standardizing authentication using WebAuthn, enterprises can provide a consistent login experience while eliminating the risks associated with password-based credentials.

Biometric authentication plays a crucial role in enterprise passwordless IAM, providing a user-friendly and highly secure alternative to traditional authentication mechanisms. Biometrics leverage unique physiological characteristics, such as fingerprints, facial recognition, iris scans, and voice recognition, to authenticate users without requiring passwords. Modern devices, including smartphones, laptops, and tablets, come equipped with biometric sensors that support native authentication frameworks like Windows Hello, Apple Face ID, and

Android Biometrics API. Enterprises should integrate biometric authentication with IAM platforms to enable seamless, passwordless login experiences for employees, partners, and customers.

To ensure security and privacy in biometric authentication, enterprises must implement strong data protection measures. Unlike passwords, biometric templates cannot be easily changed if compromised, making secure storage and processing critical. FIDO2-compliant biometric authentication ensures that biometric data is never transmitted or stored centrally, reducing the risk of biometric data breaches. Instead, biometric credentials are stored locally on user devices, where authentication occurs in a secure enclave, such as Apple's Secure Enclave, Microsoft's TPM (Trusted Platform Module), or Android's StrongBox. Implementing biometric authentication with decentralized storage enhances security while ensuring compliance with privacy regulations such as GDPR and CCPA.

Hardware-based authentication devices, including security keys and smart cards, provide an additional layer of security in enterprise passwordless IAM. FIDO2 security keys, such as YubiKey and Google Titan, enable strong authentication by generating cryptographic signatures that verify user identity without requiring passwords. These hardware-based authenticators support multi-factor authentication (MFA) by combining something the user has (a security key) with something the user is (biometric authentication) or something the user knows (a PIN). Enterprises should deploy security keys as a passwordless authentication option for high-security use cases, such as privileged access management (PAM) and administrative account authentication.

Adaptive authentication enhances passwordless IAM by dynamically adjusting authentication requirements based on contextual risk signals. Unlike static authentication policies, which apply the same authentication method to all users, adaptive authentication evaluates factors such as user behavior, device trust, location, and login anomalies to determine the appropriate level of authentication. If a user logs in from a trusted device in a familiar location, passwordless authentication via biometrics or a security key may be sufficient. However, if an anomalous login attempt is detected—such as an access request from an untrusted network or a new device—adaptive authentication can enforce additional verification steps, such as a second biometric factor or a step-up security challenge.

Implementing passwordless IAM at an enterprise scale requires seamless integration with existing identity infrastructure. Legacy applications, mainframe systems, and on-premises Active Directory environments often rely on traditional authentication mechanisms that do not natively support passwordless authentication. Enterprises must adopt modern authentication protocols, such as OpenID Connect (OIDC) and OAuth2, to enable passwordless authentication across cloud and on-premises environments. Identity federation plays a crucial role in extending passwordless authentication to third-party applications, ensuring that users can authenticate once using a FIDO2 credential and gain access to multiple enterprise resources without re-entering passwords.

Passwordless IAM also enhances security posture by eliminating the risks associated with password-based attacks. Traditional phishing attacks trick users into revealing passwords, but FIDO2 and biometric authentication are resistant to such threats because authentication occurs locally and credentials are never transmitted. Additionally, passwordless authentication reduces the attack surface for brute-force and credential stuffing attacks, which exploit weak or reused passwords. By eliminating passwords, enterprises mitigate common security threats while simplifying user authentication workflows.

Regulatory compliance and industry standards increasingly emphasize strong authentication mechanisms, making passwordless IAM a strategic priority for enterprises. Regulations such as the Payment Services Directive 2 (PSD2), the National Institute of Standards and Technology (NIST) 800-63B, and the Cybersecurity Maturity Model Certification (CMMC) mandate the use of multi-factor authentication (MFA) and phishing-resistant authentication methods. FIDO2 and biometric authentication align with these security requirements, enabling enterprises to achieve compliance while improving authentication security. Implementing passwordless authentication reduces the burden of password management audits, password rotation policies, and account recovery processes, streamlining compliance efforts.

A key consideration in passwordless IAM adoption is user experience and change management. Enterprises transitioning to passwordless authentication must ensure that users understand the benefits, trust the security mechanisms, and adopt new authentication workflows seamlessly. User education programs, intuitive onboarding processes, and self-service authentication management portals help drive passwordless adoption. Providing multiple passwordless authentication options, including biometrics, security keys, and device-based authentication, ensures flexibility and accessibility for diverse user populations.

Enterprises must continuously monitor and optimize their passwordless IAM implementations to ensure security effectiveness and user satisfaction. Security teams should analyze authentication logs, monitor biometric authentication trends, and assess the adoption of FIDO2 credentials to refine authentication policies. Integrating passwordless authentication with Security Information and Event Management (SIEM) solutions enables real-time threat detection and response, ensuring that authentication anomalies are identified and mitigated promptly.

By architecting a passwordless IAM framework that integrates FIDO2, biometric authentication, adaptive security, and identity federation, enterprises can enhance security, reduce password-related risks, and improve the authentication experience. As passwordless authentication continues to gain industry adoption, organizations that embrace this transformation will achieve stronger security resilience while eliminating one of the most persistent vulnerabilities in enterprise IAM: passwords.

IAM Performance Optimization at Scale: High Throughput and Low Latency Designs

Identity and Access Management (IAM) systems serve as the foundation for authentication, authorization, and identity governance in modern enterprises. As organizations scale to millions of users, applications, and devices, IAM performance optimization becomes critical to ensuring seamless access while maintaining security. High throughput and low latency are essential design principles for IAM systems that must process millions of authentication requests per second, enforce fine-grained authorization policies in real time, and synchronize identities across multi-cloud environments. Without a well-architected IAM performance strategy, authentication bottlenecks, slow authorization decisions, and latency issues can disrupt business operations, degrade user experience, and expose security risks.

High-performance IAM architectures must prioritize scalability by implementing distributed, stateless authentication services that handle requests efficiently. Traditional monolithic IAM systems that rely on centralized identity stores create performance bottlenecks as authentication traffic increases. Instead, organizations should adopt microservices-based IAM architectures that distribute authentication workloads across multiple regions, data centers, and cloud providers. Stateless authentication mechanisms, such as JSON Web Tokens (JWTs) and OAuth2 access tokens, reduce the need for session persistence and database lookups, enabling IAM services to scale horizontally without sacrificing performance.

Load balancing plays a crucial role in IAM performance optimization, ensuring that authentication and authorization requests are evenly distributed across IAM nodes. Enterprises should deploy global load balancers, such as AWS Elastic Load Balancing (ELB), Azure Traffic Manager, or Google Cloud Load Balancing, to route identity requests to the nearest available authentication server. Local load balancing within IAM clusters further optimizes performance by dynamically allocating authentication workloads based on server health, request latency, and regional traffic patterns. Implementing auto-scaling mechanisms ensures that IAM services can dynamically scale up during peak authentication periods and scale down during low-traffic intervals, optimizing resource utilization while maintaining availability.

Caching strategies are essential for reducing IAM latency and improving request processing speed. Caching frequently accessed identity attributes, authentication tokens, and authorization decisions eliminates redundant database queries, improving response times for high-volume authentication transactions. Enterprises should leverage distributed caching solutions such as Redis, Memcached, or AWS ElastiCache to store authentication tokens and authorization decisions close to IAM processing nodes. Implementing token introspection caches ensures that OAuth2 and OpenID Connect (OIDC) tokens are validated efficiently without introducing database overhead. Additionally, caching group memberships, role assignments, and attribute-based access control (ABAC) evaluations minimizes authorization processing delays, ensuring low-latency access control enforcement.

Database performance optimization is critical for IAM scalability, as authentication and authorization workflows rely on fast identity lookups, attribute resolution, and policy enforcement. Traditional relational databases can become a bottleneck as IAM workloads grow, necessitating the adoption of optimized database architectures. NoSQL databases such as Amazon DynamoDB, Google Firestore, and Azure Cosmos DB offer high availability, low-latency data retrieval, and scalable performance for IAM use cases. Implementing multi-master database replication ensures that identity records are synchronized across regions, reducing latency for globally distributed IAM deployments. Database indexing, query optimization, and read replicas further enhance IAM performance by minimizing query response times and improving data retrieval efficiency.

IAM performance at scale also depends on optimizing authentication protocol efficiency. Traditional authentication mechanisms that require multiple back-and-forth exchanges between clients and IAM servers introduce latency, especially in global deployments. Protocol optimizations such as reducing the number of HTTP round trips in OAuth2 flows, implementing short-lived session tokens, and leveraging client-side token storage improve authentication efficiency. Single Sign-On (SSO) federation using SAML, OpenID Connect, and OAuth2 should be optimized to minimize token validation delays and reduce dependency on remote identity providers. By fine-tuning authentication protocols, organizations can ensure rapid user authentication while maintaining strong security controls.

API rate limiting and throttling mechanisms are essential for protecting IAM services from performance degradation due to excessive authentication requests. Enterprises should enforce rate limits on IAM APIs using API gateways such as AWS API Gateway, Azure API Management, and Google Apigee. Implementing request quotas, burst limits, and dynamic throttling policies prevents IAM services from being overwhelmed by high-frequency requests, ensuring fair resource allocation across all clients. Rate-limited authentication flows, combined with exponential backoff strategies for failed authentication attempts, reduce unnecessary IAM load while preventing denial-of-service (DoS) attacks.

IAM resilience is a key factor in performance optimization, ensuring continuous authentication availability even during infrastructure failures or network disruptions. Implementing geographically distributed IAM deployments with active-active failover capabilities ensures high availability and fault tolerance. Multi-region IAM clusters, DNS-based failover strategies, and hybrid IAM architectures that operate across cloud and on-premises environments provide redundancy and load balancing, reducing the risk of authentication failures. By designing IAM systems with built-in resilience, organizations minimize downtime and ensure consistent performance across global user bases.

Optimizing authorization performance is equally important in IAM scalability. Fine-grained access control models, such as ABAC and PBAC, require dynamic policy evaluations that can introduce latency if not optimized. Enterprises should implement precomputed access control decisions, policy caching, and real-time policy evaluation engines to streamline authorization workflows. Policy enforcement points (PEPs) should be distributed across application endpoints to reduce authorization processing delays, ensuring that access control decisions are executed as close to the request source as possible. Policy engines such as Open Policy Agent (OPA) and XACML-based access control frameworks should be optimized for high-performance rule evaluation, ensuring that access decisions are made with minimal delay.

IAM monitoring and observability are critical for identifying performance bottlenecks and optimizing system efficiency. Implementing real-time IAM analytics using OpenTelemetry, Fluentd, and Prometheus enables organizations to monitor authentication response times, API latencies, and policy evaluation performance. Security Information and Event Management (SIEM) platforms, such as Splunk, Azure Sentinel, and Google Chronicle, provide identity activity insights, helping security teams detect anomalies and optimize IAM workflows. Continuous performance testing, stress testing, and synthetic monitoring ensure that IAM systems can handle peak authentication loads while maintaining low-latency access control enforcement.

Continuous optimization of IAM performance requires automation and Infrastructure-as-Code (IaC) approaches. Deploying IAM services using Kubernetes, Terraform, and AWS CloudFormation ensures repeatable and scalable IAM infrastructure. Automating IAM performance tuning, including auto-scaling IAM nodes, optimizing database queries, and dynamically adjusting caching policies, enhances IAM efficiency while reducing operational overhead. DevSecOps integration ensures that IAM performance optimizations align with security best practices, enabling secure and scalable authentication architectures.

By architecting IAM for high throughput and low latency, enterprises can ensure seamless authentication, rapid access control enforcement, and resilient identity services at scale. Optimizing IAM performance enhances user experience, improves system reliability, and strengthens security posture, enabling organizations to meet the demands of modern digital ecosystems. As authentication workloads continue to grow, IAM scalability and efficiency will remain critical factors in enterprise security strategy.

Advanced Identity Federation Patterns: B2B, B2C, and Government Interoperability

Identity federation has become a critical component of modern Identity and Access Management (IAM) strategies, enabling seamless authentication across multiple organizations, platforms, and jurisdictions. As enterprises, governments, and service providers expand their digital ecosystems, they must integrate disparate identity systems while maintaining security, compliance, and user experience. Advanced identity federation patterns allow organizations to establish trust relationships between different identity domains, ensuring that users can authenticate once and gain access to multiple services without requiring redundant credentials. Whether in business-to-business (B2B), business-to-consumer (B2C), or government interoperability scenarios, federated IAM architectures must be designed for scalability, flexibility, and security to support diverse identity sources and access requirements.

B2B identity federation enables secure authentication and authorization between business partners, suppliers, and third-party service providers. In traditional B2B environments, organizations manage separate identity repositories, leading to complex integration challenges, inconsistent security policies, and administrative overhead. Federation simplifies cross-organizational authentication by allowing each entity to retain control over its own identity system while enabling trust relationships with external partners. Standardized protocols such as Security Assertion Markup Language (SAML), OpenID Connect (OIDC), and OAuth2 facilitate B2B federation by allowing users to authenticate with their home organization's identity provider (IdP) while accessing partner services.

In B2B identity federation, organizations often implement a hub-and-spoke model, where a central identity broker facilitates authentication between multiple business entities. The identity broker acts as an intermediary IdP, validating authentication requests from different organizations and issuing security tokens that enable access to federated applications. This model reduces the complexity of managing multiple bilateral federation agreements and provides a scalable framework for onboarding new partners. Additionally, implementing Just-in-Time (JIT) provisioning within federated B2B ecosystems allows dynamic account creation in target applications, eliminating the need for manual user provisioning while ensuring access is granted only when necessary.

B2C identity federation extends authentication capabilities to customers, allowing them to access multiple digital services using a single identity. Unlike B2B scenarios, where identity federation focuses on enterprise integrations, B2C federation prioritizes user convenience, security, and privacy. Social login is a common B2C federation model, where users authenticate using their existing credentials from social identity providers such as Google, Facebook, Apple ID, or LinkedIn. Social identity federation reduces friction in customer onboarding while leveraging secure authentication mechanisms such as OpenID Connect (OIDC) and OAuth2.

Beyond social login, B2C identity federation also incorporates decentralized identity models, where users control their digital identities through self-sovereign identity (SSI) frameworks. Organizations adopting SSI leverage verifiable credentials (VCs) and decentralized identifiers (DIDs) to authenticate customers without requiring centralized identity repositories. Blockchain-based identity networks, such as Sovrin and the Trust Over IP (ToIP) framework, enable secure, privacy-preserving B2C federation by allowing users to present cryptographic proof of identity without disclosing unnecessary personal data. This approach aligns with regulatory requirements such as GDPR and the California Consumer Privacy Act (CCPA), which emphasize user consent and data minimization.

Government identity federation plays a crucial role in enabling secure and interoperable authentication across public sector services. Many governments operate multiple agencies, each with its own identity management system, leading to identity silos that hinder digital service delivery. Federated IAM models allow citizens, businesses, and government employees to authenticate once and access multiple government services without re-entering credentials. National identity frameworks, such as eIDAS in the European Union, NIST Digital Identity Guidelines in the United States, and Aadhaar-based authentication in India, establish standardized trust mechanisms for government-to-government (G2G), government-to-business (G2B), and government-to-citizen (G2C) identity federation.

Cross-border identity federation is particularly relevant in international trade, global mobility, and diplomatic services. Organizations participating in multinational agreements require secure identity verification mechanisms that comply with regional regulations while enabling seamless access to digital services. The eIDAS framework, for example, facilitates mutual recognition of electronic identities across EU member states, allowing citizens to authenticate with their national eID systems while accessing foreign government services. Similar initiatives, such as the Pan-Canadian Trust Framework (PCTF) and the Global Digital Identity Interoperability Framework (GDIF), aim to establish globally recognized identity federation standards.

Security and trust management are fundamental to advanced identity federation patterns. Establishing federated trust requires cryptographic signing of authentication assertions, secure token exchanges, and continuous monitoring of trust relationships. Organizations must implement identity proofing mechanisms to verify the legitimacy of federated users before granting access. Strong authentication requirements, such as multi-factor authentication (MFA) and passwordless authentication using FIDO2, further enhance security in federated environments.

Federated identity governance is essential to ensure compliance with data protection regulations and industry standards. Organizations must enforce strict policies regarding identity data sharing, consent management, and access revocation. Privacy-preserving federation techniques, such as token anonymization and zero-knowledge proofs (ZKPs), allow organizations to authenticate users without exposing personally identifiable information (PII). Integrating federated IAM with Security Information and Event Management (SIEM) and User and Entity Behavior Analytics (UEBA) enhances security monitoring by detecting anomalies in federated authentication patterns.

Multi-cloud identity federation is another critical aspect of modern IAM architectures. As enterprises adopt hybrid and multi-cloud environments, federated authentication across cloud providers becomes essential to maintaining a seamless user experience while enforcing consistent security policies. Cloud-native IAM solutions, such as AWS IAM, Azure AD B2B, and Google Cloud IAM, provide built-in federation capabilities that allow enterprises to integrate multiple cloud services without creating duplicate identities. Workload identity federation extends this capability to applications and APIs, enabling secure authentication of cloud-native workloads across different cloud platforms.

The success of identity federation depends on interoperability and adherence to open standards. Organizations implementing federated IAM should follow best practices, including adopting identity federation frameworks such as the Kantara Initiative, the OpenID Foundation, and the FIDO Alliance. Standardizing identity federation policies, authentication protocols, and attribute mapping strategies ensures that identity federation remains scalable, secure, and future-proof.

Advanced identity federation patterns enable organizations to extend secure authentication beyond traditional enterprise boundaries, facilitating seamless access for business partners, customers, and government entities. By leveraging federation models such as hub-and-spoke, social login, self-sovereign identity, and cross-border authentication frameworks, organizations can enhance security, streamline identity management, and improve user experience across interconnected digital ecosystems. As the demand for frictionless authentication and regulatory compliance grows, federated IAM architectures will continue to evolve, shaping the future of secure and interoperable digital identity.

IAM Threat Models: Architecting Defenses Against Advanced Identity Attacks

Identity and Access Management (IAM) is a primary target for cyber threats, as compromised identities provide attackers with direct access to critical enterprise resources. Threat actors continuously evolve their tactics, leveraging sophisticated attack vectors to exploit weaknesses in authentication mechanisms, authorization controls, and identity governance processes. Organizations must adopt a proactive approach to IAM security by developing robust threat models that identify vulnerabilities, simulate attack scenarios, and implement layered defenses to mitigate risks. Effective IAM threat modeling enables security teams to anticipate emerging threats, harden identity infrastructure, and minimize the attack surface across cloud, hybrid, and on-premises environments.

Credential-based attacks remain one of the most significant threats to IAM systems. Phishing, credential stuffing, and password spraying attacks exploit weak authentication practices, allowing adversaries to gain unauthorized access to enterprise applications. Attackers use social engineering techniques to trick users into revealing credentials, while automated tools test stolen password databases against multiple accounts to identify reused credentials. To defend against credential-based threats, organizations must implement phishing-resistant authentication mechanisms, such as FIDO2-based passwordless authentication, hardware security keys, and biometric authentication. Enforcing Multi-Factor Authentication (MFA) with adaptive risk-based authentication further strengthens IAM defenses by requiring additional verification for high-risk login attempts.

Session hijacking and token theft attacks target authentication mechanisms by intercepting or manipulating session tokens. Attackers exploit insecure storage of tokens, weak session management practices, and token replay vulnerabilities to impersonate legitimate users. OAuth2 and OpenID Connect (OIDC) token theft can occur when attackers compromise client secrets, authorization codes, or refresh tokens. To mitigate session hijacking risks, IAM architectures must enforce short-lived session tokens, implement secure token storage using encrypted hardware enclaves, and validate token integrity through introspection endpoints. Deploying OAuth2 Proof Key for Code Exchange (PKCE) prevents authorization code interception in public client flows, while enforcing mTLS (mutual TLS) authentication secures token exchanges between microservices and APIs.

Privilege escalation attacks exploit misconfigured IAM policies, excessive permissions, and role abuse to elevate user privileges beyond intended access levels. Attackers leverage permission gaps in cloud IAM policies, improperly assigned administrator roles, and overly permissive service accounts to gain unauthorized access to critical infrastructure. Cloud IAM misconfigurations, such as excessive AWS IAM roles, overly broad Google Cloud IAM bindings, or Azure Active Directory (Azure AD) privilege misassignments, expose enterprises to privilege escalation risks. Implementing least privilege access principles, Just-in-Time (JIT) access provisioning, and automated IAM policy audits help organizations prevent privilege escalation attacks.

Cloud Security Posture Management (CSPM) and Identity Threat Detection and Response (ITDR) tools continuously monitor IAM configurations, flagging excessive permissions and unauthorized privilege escalations.

Insider threats pose a significant challenge to IAM security, as employees, contractors, and privileged users may abuse legitimate access for malicious purposes. Insider threats range from intentional data exfiltration and financial fraud to accidental privilege misuse. Traditional IAM systems often lack real-time visibility into abnormal user behavior, making it difficult to detect insider threats before damage occurs. Organizations must integrate IAM with User and Entity Behavior Analytics (UEBA) to detect deviations from normal access patterns, flagging unusual privilege escalations, excessive data downloads, and unauthorized access attempts. Implementing just-enough-access (JEA) policies, role-based risk scoring, and continuous identity analytics reduces the likelihood of insider-driven IAM compromises.

Identity federation and Single Sign-On (SSO) introduce new threat vectors, including identity provider (IdP) compromise, trust misconfigurations, and federation token manipulation. Attackers who breach an IdP can generate fraudulent authentication assertions, granting unauthorized access to federated applications. Cross-domain identity federation expands the attack surface, as weaknesses in one federated domain may be exploited to compromise others. To secure identity federation, enterprises must enforce strong cryptographic signing of SAML and OIDC assertions, implement identity provider isolation strategies, and conduct continuous validation of federated trust relationships. Secure Assertion Markup Language (SAML) response validation, audience restriction enforcement, and Just-In-Time (JIT) provisioning monitoring further strengthen federated IAM security.

API key abuse and machine identity threats target service-to-service authentication mechanisms, exploiting weak API key management practices and misconfigured service accounts. Attackers who obtain API credentials can execute unauthorized API calls, exfiltrate sensitive data, and manipulate cloud workloads. Machine identities, including IoT devices, service accounts, and containerized workloads, often have excessive permissions that increase the risk of compromise. Organizations must implement workload identity federation using short-lived, just-in-time API credentials instead of static API keys. Securing service-to-service authentication with mTLS, OAuth2 client credentials flow, and policy-based access controls (PBAC) ensures that machine identities operate within strict security boundaries.

Man-in-the-middle (MITM) attacks exploit insecure authentication channels, intercepting login credentials, session tokens, and authorization codes. Attackers use phishing proxies, rogue Wi-Fi networks, and TLS stripping techniques to manipulate authentication flows. IAM architectures must enforce end-to-end encryption using TLS 1.3, implement DNS-based authentication of named entities (DANE) to prevent TLS downgrades, and adopt certificate pinning to mitigate MITM threats. Secure WebAuthn authentication over FIDO2-compliant devices eliminates credential interception risks by ensuring that authentication occurs locally on a user's trusted device.

IAM resilience must also address Distributed Denial-of-Service (DDoS) attacks targeting authentication endpoints. Large-scale authentication requests, automated login attempts, and API abuse can overload IAM infrastructure, causing authentication failures and service disruptions. Rate limiting, CAPTCHA-based bot detection, and AI-driven anomaly detection mitigate IAM DDoS risks by blocking automated attacks while allowing legitimate traffic. Implementing IAM request throttling policies, edge-based authentication caching, and identity-aware rate controls ensures that IAM services remain available under high-traffic conditions.

Account takeover (ATO) attacks leverage credential compromise, session hijacking, and social engineering to gain control over user accounts. Attackers use credential stuffing, brute-force password guessing, and SIM swapping attacks to bypass authentication mechanisms. IAM threat models must incorporate continuous authentication strategies that assess user risk throughout a session. Behavioral biometrics, geolocation-based anomaly detection, and step-up authentication workflows dynamically adjust security controls to prevent ATO attacks. Integrating IAM with identity fraud detection platforms further enhances defenses by identifying compromised credentials and blocking high-risk login attempts before they result in account takeovers.

IAM threat modeling requires continuous evaluation, attack simulation, and red teaming exercises to identify weaknesses in identity security controls. Organizations should conduct IAM penetration testing, adversary-in-the-middle simulations, and cloud IAM misconfiguration assessments to validate their identity security posture. Implementing automated IAM security baselines, real-time identity monitoring, and AI-driven identity threat response enhances overall IAM resilience against advanced cyber threats.

By architecting IAM defenses against sophisticated identity attacks, organizations can safeguard authentication workflows, enforce least privilege access, and prevent identity compromise across cloud, hybrid, and on-premises environments. As identity threats continue to evolve, IAM security must remain adaptive, intelligence-driven, and deeply integrated with enterprise cybersecurity frameworks.

Architecting Machine Identity Management and Workload IAM

Machine identities have become a critical aspect of modern Identity and Access Management (IAM), as enterprises increasingly rely on cloud computing, microservices, IoT devices, and automated workloads. Unlike human users, machine identities do not follow traditional authentication and authorization processes but require secure, scalable, and automated identity lifecycle management. Without proper governance, machine identities can introduce security risks, such as credential sprawl, overprivileged service accounts, and unauthorized API access. Architecting a robust Machine Identity Management (MIM) and Workload IAM framework ensures that applications, services, and infrastructure components can authenticate securely, establish trust, and enforce fine-grained access controls across hybrid and multi-cloud environments.

Machine identities encompass a wide range of non-human entities, including virtual machines, cloud workloads, containers, IoT devices, APIs, and serverless functions. These identities authenticate and interact with each other through secure certificates, API keys, OAuth2 client credentials, and workload federation mechanisms. Unlike human identities, which are managed through directories and authentication protocols such as SAML or OpenID Connect (OIDC), machine identities rely on cryptographic credentials and dynamic identity providers that ensure seamless communication without manual intervention. Enterprises must implement automated machine identity issuance, rotation, and revocation processes to maintain security and prevent unauthorized access.

One of the key challenges in Machine Identity Management is securing service-to-service authentication in distributed environments. Traditional IAM models, which rely on static credentials such as hardcoded API keys, SSH keys, and plaintext secrets, are prone to compromise and unauthorized usage. Attackers who gain access to exposed credentials can execute privileged operations, exfiltrate sensitive data, and manipulate cloud workloads. To mitigate these risks, enterprises must adopt dynamic, short-lived machine identities that authenticate using mutual TLS (mTLS), workload identity federation, and just-in-time credential issuance. By eliminating long-lived credentials, organizations reduce the attack surface while improving security posture.

Workload identity federation is essential for enabling secure, cross-cloud authentication without relying on static credentials. Cloud-native identity services such as AWS IAM Roles for Service Accounts (IRSA), Google Cloud Workload Identity Federation, and Azure Managed Identities allow workloads to authenticate using federated identity providers instead of traditional API keys. This approach ensures that machine identities inherit security policies dynamically, reducing the complexity of managing credentials across multi-cloud environments. By leveraging OpenID Connect (OIDC)-based workload federation, enterprises enable secure, policy-driven authentication for Kubernetes clusters, serverless functions, and cloud-native workloads.

Authorization for machine identities must be carefully designed to enforce least privilege access and prevent privilege escalation attacks.

Unlike human users, machines often require access to multiple systems, databases, and APIs to perform automated tasks. Overprivileged machine identities pose a significant security risk, as compromised service accounts can be exploited to move laterally across cloud environments. Implementing Attribute-Based Access Control (ABAC) and Policy-Based Access Control (PBAC) ensures that machine identities only receive the minimum required permissions based on real-time context, workload attributes, and operational risk factors. Access policies should be dynamically evaluated using policy engines such as Open Policy Agent (OPA) or cloud-native IAM policy frameworks.

Machine identity lifecycle management must be automated to prevent credential sprawl and unauthorized persistence of service accounts. Enterprises should implement automated identity provisioning, key rotation, and revocation workflows to ensure that machine identities are continuously managed and aligned with security policies. Certificate-based authentication using PKI (Public Key Infrastructure) enhances security by ensuring that machine identities are issued and revoked dynamically based on trust policies. Secrets management platforms such as HashiCorp Vault, AWS Secrets Manager, and Azure Key Vault play a crucial role in securely storing and rotating machine identity credentials, eliminating hardcoded secrets in application code.

Auditing and monitoring of machine identities are essential for detecting anomalies, unauthorized access, and credential misuse. Unlike human authentication logs, which provide clear identity attribution, machine authentication events can be challenging to interpret without proper logging and correlation mechanisms. Organizations must integrate Machine Identity Management with Security Information and Event Management (SIEM) solutions to track workload authentication patterns, identify suspicious API calls, and enforce anomaly detection. Implementing User and Entity Behavior Analytics (UEBA) further enhances security by analyzing workload activity baselines and flagging deviations that may indicate compromised machine identities.

Scaling Machine Identity Management across hybrid and multi-cloud environments requires interoperability between different IAM systems. Enterprises operating in multi-cloud architectures must ensure that machine identities are portable across AWS, Azure, Google Cloud, and on-premises data centers. Standardizing on open authentication protocols such as OAuth2, SPIFFE (Secure Production Identity Framework for Everyone), and X.509 certificates ensures that workload IAM policies remain consistent across different platforms. Implementing a federated identity management approach for workloads allows organizations to maintain a unified trust model while enforcing security controls at the cloud-native level.

Serverless architectures introduce new challenges in Machine Identity Management, as serverless functions execute transient workloads that require secure authentication and authorization without persistent identities. Traditional IAM models, which rely on long-lived credentials, do not scale effectively in ephemeral computing environments. Organizations must implement event-driven identity policies that grant just-in-time credentials to serverless functions based on request context and runtime security constraints. By leveraging cloud-native IAM services such as AWS Lambda IAM Roles, Azure Functions Managed Identities, and Google Cloud Service Accounts, enterprises ensure that serverless workloads authenticate securely without exposing sensitive credentials.

IoT device identity management is another critical aspect of Machine Identity Management, as billions of connected devices require secure authentication and encrypted communication channels. IoT IAM solutions must support hardware-based device authentication, zero-trust access policies, and dynamic certificate issuance. Implementing mutual authentication between IoT devices and cloud platforms ensures that only authorized devices can interact with enterprise systems. By leveraging IoT IAM frameworks such as AWS IoT Core, Azure IoT Hub, and Google Cloud IoT, organizations can enforce secure identity lifecycle management for connected devices while mitigating risks associated with unauthorized device access.

Machine identity governance must align with enterprise IAM strategies to ensure compliance with security regulations such as GDPR, PCI-DSS, and NIST 800-63. Organizations must implement machine identity access reviews, risk-based policy enforcement, and periodic privilege audits to maintain security and compliance. Automating identity governance through policy-driven workflows ensures that machine identities adhere to security best practices while reducing administrative overhead.

By architecting a comprehensive Machine Identity Management framework, enterprises can secure workload authentication, enforce least privilege access, and prevent credential compromise in cloud-native environments. A well-designed workload IAM strategy integrates identity federation, dynamic authorization, secrets management, and continuous monitoring to safeguard machine identities against evolving cyber threats. As enterprises continue adopting automation, cloud computing, and IoT technologies, Machine Identity Management will remain a cornerstone of modern IAM architectures, enabling secure and scalable authentication for non-human entities.

Identity Fabric: Unifying IAM Across Cloud, On-Prem, and SaaS

Modern enterprises operate in complex environments that span on-premises infrastructure, multiple cloud providers, and an expanding ecosystem of Software-as-a-Service (SaaS) applications. Managing identity and access consistently across these heterogeneous environments is a fundamental challenge for Identity and Access Management (IAM) teams. Identity silos, fragmented authentication mechanisms, and inconsistent access control policies create security risks, operational inefficiencies, and compliance challenges. The concept of Identity Fabric addresses these challenges by providing a unified, flexible, and context-aware IAM framework that integrates identities across all enterprise environments.

Identity Fabric is not a single technology but rather an architectural approach that enables seamless identity interoperability across diverse IT ecosystems. It provides a consolidated identity management layer that abstracts identity providers, authentication protocols, and access policies, ensuring that users and machines can authenticate and interact with enterprise resources securely, regardless of where they reside. By implementing an Identity Fabric, organizations can enforce consistent security policies, streamline identity governance, and improve user experience across cloud, on-premises, and SaaS applications.

A key component of Identity Fabric is federated identity management, which enables users to authenticate once and access multiple applications without needing separate credentials. Federated authentication using Security Assertion Markup Language (SAML), OpenID Connect (OIDC), and OAuth2 ensures that identities can be verified across different environments while maintaining a centralized trust model. Enterprises must integrate cloud-based identity providers (IdPs) such as Azure AD, Okta, and Google Cloud Identity with legacy on-premises directories like Active Directory (AD) and LDAP to create a seamless authentication experience. By implementing Single Sign-On (SSO) across all identity domains, organizations eliminate the need for multiple login credentials while enforcing strong authentication policies.

An effective Identity Fabric architecture also supports adaptive authentication and risk-based access control. Traditional authentication models apply static policies, which fail to account for real-time security threats and changing user contexts. Identity Fabric enables adaptive authentication by analyzing user behavior, device trust, location, and risk signals before granting access. If a user attempts to authenticate from an unusual location or an untrusted device, the system can enforce step-up authentication, requiring additional verification such as biometrics or a security key. This context-aware approach enhances security while reducing authentication friction for trusted users.

Identity governance and administration (IGA) must be seamlessly integrated into an Identity Fabric to maintain visibility and control over user identities, entitlements, and access reviews. Organizations must implement automated identity lifecycle management processes to provision, modify, and revoke access across on-premises systems, cloud applications, and SaaS platforms in real time. Integrating IGA solutions with HR systems and IT service management (ITSM) platforms ensures that user access aligns with job roles and organizational policies. Periodic access certification reviews and real-time entitlement monitoring help prevent excessive permissions and unauthorized access, reducing the risk of insider threats.

Managing machine identities is another critical aspect of Identity Fabric. Modern enterprises rely on non-human entities, including cloud workloads, microservices, IoT devices, and automated scripts, all of which require authentication and secure access to enterprise resources. Unlike human identities, which rely on passwords and multi-factor authentication, machine identities use cryptographic credentials, certificates, and API tokens for authentication. Identity Fabric must integrate with machine identity management platforms, such as AWS IAM Roles, Azure Managed Identities, and Google Workload Identity Federation, to ensure that workloads can authenticate dynamically without exposing static credentials. By enforcing just-in-time (JIT) access policies for machine identities, enterprises can prevent privilege misuse and unauthorized API access.

Hybrid IAM architectures must support seamless synchronization of identity attributes across on-premises directories, cloud identity stores, and SaaS applications. Many enterprises still rely on legacy Active Directory environments while adopting cloud-first strategies, leading to identity fragmentation. Identity Fabric enables real-time synchronization of user attributes, group memberships, and access policies across hybrid environments, ensuring that identity data remains consistent and up to date. Implementing cloud identity synchronization tools, such as Azure AD Connect, Google Cloud Directory Sync, or Okta Universal Directory, eliminates identity silos and enhances interoperability between on-premises and cloud-based IAM systems.

Zero Trust principles must be embedded within an Identity Fabric to ensure that access decisions are continuously evaluated based on real-time security signals. Traditional perimeter-based security models assume implicit trust for users inside corporate networks, but this approach fails in modern hybrid and cloud environments. Identity Fabric enforces Zero Trust by requiring continuous identity verification, least privilege access, and micro-segmentation for both human and machine identities. Integrating IAM with endpoint security, SIEM (Security Information and Event Management), and threat intelligence platforms allows organizations to detect and respond to identity-based threats in real time.

Privileged Access Management (PAM) plays a crucial role in securing administrative access within an Identity Fabric. Privileged accounts, such as system administrators, DevOps engineers, and cloud administrators, have elevated permissions that pose a significant security risk if compromised. Traditional PAM solutions focus on on-premises environments, but in a hybrid IAM architecture, privileged access must extend to cloud workloads and SaaS applications. Identity Fabric integrates with cloud-native PAM solutions, enabling just-in-time privileged access, session monitoring, and automated privilege escalation policies. By enforcing least privilege access and continuously monitoring privileged sessions, organizations reduce the risk of insider threats and credential compromise.

IAM performance and scalability are essential for implementing a high-performing Identity Fabric that can support millions of authentication requests and authorization decisions in real time. Identity workloads must be distributed across multiple regions to minimize latency and ensure high availability. Implementing load balancing, caching strategies, and distributed IAM clusters ensures that authentication services can handle peak traffic loads while maintaining low response times. Integrating IAM with Content Delivery Networks (CDNs) and edge authentication proxies further enhances performance by reducing authentication round trips for globally distributed users.

Compliance and regulatory requirements must also be addressed within an Identity Fabric. Enterprises operating in multiple jurisdictions must comply with data sovereignty laws, such as GDPR, CCPA, and the China Cybersecurity Law, which impose strict requirements on identity data storage and processing. Identity Fabric must enforce regional compliance policies, ensuring that identity data is stored within authorized geographic boundaries while enabling federated authentication across jurisdictions. Implementing privacy-preserving identity federation, consent management frameworks, and automated compliance reporting ensures that IAM remains aligned with regulatory mandates.

An effective Identity Fabric strategy must also focus on user experience and operational efficiency. Frictionless authentication, self-service identity management portals, and delegated administration capabilities improve IAM usability for employees, customers, and partners. Providing users with a unified access portal that consolidates cloud, on-premises, and SaaS applications enhances productivity while reducing IT support costs. Automating IAM workflows, access approvals, and identity governance processes minimizes administrative overhead and accelerates digital transformation initiatives.

By architecting an Identity Fabric that unifies IAM across cloud, on-premises, and SaaS environments, organizations achieve greater security, operational agility, and compliance readiness. Identity Fabric enables seamless authentication, dynamic access control, and centralized identity governance, ensuring that enterprises can manage identities efficiently while adapting to evolving cybersecurity threats and business requirements. As identity ecosystems continue to grow in complexity, a well-designed Identity Fabric becomes essential for securing digital interactions and enabling a frictionless, scalable IAM framework.

Fine-Grained Authorization Architectures: ABAC, ReBAC, and Continuous Authorization

Modern enterprises require sophisticated authorization architectures to enforce precise access control policies across dynamic and distributed environments. Traditional Role-Based Access Control (RBAC) models, while widely adopted, often lack the flexibility needed to support real-time decision-making, contextual access policies, and dynamic relationships between users and resources. Fine-grained authorization architectures leverage Attribute-Based Access Control (ABAC), Relationship-Based Access Control (ReBAC), and Continuous Authorization to ensure that access decisions are context-aware, adaptive, and enforceable at scale. Implementing these advanced authorization models enables organizations to minimize overprovisioned privileges, reduce insider threats, and comply with regulatory mandates while maintaining operational agility.

Attribute-Based Access Control (ABAC) enhances authorization by evaluating access requests based on dynamic attributes rather than static roles. In an ABAC model, access control policies consider attributes related to users, resources, environment, and actions to determine whether access should be granted. User attributes may include department, job title, security clearance, or risk score, while resource attributes define sensitivity levels, ownership, or classification. Environmental attributes, such as device type, network location, time of day, or session context, provide additional security layers by adapting access decisions to real-time conditions. By incorporating ABAC into authorization architectures, organizations achieve fine-grained control over access policies while reducing the complexity associated with managing static role hierarchies.

One of the primary advantages of ABAC is its ability to support dynamic access policies that align with business needs and regulatory requirements. Unlike RBAC, which requires predefined role assignments, ABAC policies allow for real-time policy evaluation based on changing conditions. For example, a healthcare system using ABAC can grant a doctor access to patient records only if the doctor is assigned to the patient's care team and is accessing the system from a hospital-approved device. If the doctor attempts to access records from an untrusted network, the system can enforce step-up authentication or deny access altogether. ABAC enables organizations to implement least privilege access dynamically, reducing the risk of privilege creep and unauthorized data exposure.

Relationship-Based Access Control (ReBAC) extends the principles of ABAC by incorporating relationships between users, resources, and entities into authorization decisions. ReBAC is particularly valuable in environments where access control depends on complex user relationships, such as social networks, collaborative applications, and multi-tenant SaaS platforms. In ReBAC models, access policies evaluate relationships such as ownership, hierarchy, group membership, or project association to determine whether a user should be granted permissions. Unlike RBAC, which relies on predefined roles, and ABAC, which focuses on attribute evaluation, ReBAC models adapt to changing organizational structures and user interactions in real time.

One of the most common use cases for ReBAC is access control in document-sharing platforms. In a ReBAC-enabled system, a user may have access to a document if they are the document owner, a designated collaborator, or a member of a shared project team. This model ensures that access policies remain flexible and scalable, supporting dynamic permission changes without requiring manual role updates. Enterprises adopting ReBAC can implement fine-grained authorization policies that mirror real-world business relationships while maintaining strong security controls.

Continuous Authorization further strengthens fine-grained access control by enforcing real-time access decisions throughout a user session. Traditional authorization models evaluate access permissions at login or when a request is made, but they do not continuously assess security conditions after access has been granted. Continuous Authorization introduces ongoing policy enforcement that dynamically adjusts access based on real-time risk assessments, behavioral analytics, and environmental changes.

In a Continuous Authorization model, access decisions are continuously re-evaluated based on factors such as session activity, geolocation changes, or abnormal behavior patterns. For example, if a user authenticates successfully but later moves to a high-risk location or attempts an unusual data export, the system can revoke access, enforce re-authentication, or restrict permissions. Continuous Authorization mitigates the risk of session hijacking, insider threats, and compromised accounts by ensuring that security policies remain adaptive and responsive to evolving risks.

Integrating ABAC, ReBAC, and Continuous Authorization into enterprise IAM architectures requires robust policy management frameworks and scalable enforcement mechanisms. Organizations must implement policy decision points (PDPs) that evaluate access requests in real time and policy enforcement points (PEPs) that enforce access control at the application, API, or infrastructure layer. Open-source policy engines such as Open Policy Agent (OPA) and XACML-based authorization frameworks enable organizations to define, evaluate, and enforce fine-grained access policies consistently across distributed environments.

Fine-grained authorization architectures must also support delegated administration and policy abstraction to simplify access governance. Administrators should be able to define high-level policies that automatically translate into granular access controls based on contextual factors. Implementing policy-driven access governance ensures that security teams can enforce enterprise-wide access policies without manually configuring permissions for each individual user or application.

Auditing and monitoring are critical components of fine-grained authorization frameworks. Organizations must continuously track access control decisions, policy changes, and user activity to detect anomalies and enforce compliance requirements. Integrating authorization logs with Security Information and Event Management (SIEM) platforms enhances threat detection by identifying suspicious access patterns, privilege escalation attempts, and unauthorized resource modifications. By leveraging AI-driven analytics and machine learning, organizations can proactively identify and mitigate access risks before they escalate into security incidents.

Compliance with regulatory frameworks such as GDPR, HIPAA, and PCI-DSS necessitates the adoption of fine-grained authorization models that enforce strict data access policies. ABAC, ReBAC, and Continuous Authorization enable organizations to implement regulatory-compliant access controls that align with least privilege principles, data minimization requirements, and auditability mandates. By ensuring that access decisions are dynamically enforced based on real-time security conditions, enterprises can enhance regulatory compliance while improving security posture.

Enterprises deploying fine-grained authorization architectures must also focus on scalability and performance optimization. Traditional authorization mechanisms that rely on centralized policy evaluation can introduce latency and processing overhead, especially in high-traffic environments. To mitigate performance bottlenecks, organizations should implement distributed policy enforcement models that leverage edge computing, caching strategies, and real-time policy evaluation engines. Cloud-native IAM architectures must integrate fine-grained authorization at the API gateway and service mesh layers to ensure seamless policy enforcement across microservices and serverless functions.

By architecting fine-grained authorization frameworks that incorporate ABAC, ReBAC, and Continuous Authorization, organizations achieve highly adaptive access control models that enhance security, reduce administrative complexity, and improve compliance readiness. Implementing dynamic access policies, contextual risk evaluation, and real-time enforcement mechanisms enables enterprises to manage access with precision while minimizing the risks associated with static role-based models. As identity threats continue to evolve, fine-grained authorization architectures will remain a cornerstone of modern IAM strategies, ensuring that access control policies are resilient, scalable, and aligned with business objectives.

IAM in Microservices: API-Driven Identity and Service-to-Service Authentication

Identity and Access Management (IAM) in microservices architectures presents unique challenges compared to traditional monolithic applications. In a microservices environment, authentication and authorization must be distributed, scalable, and API-driven to support thousands of independent services communicating across cloud and hybrid infrastructures. Unlike monolithic systems, where IAM is typically centralized and session-based, microservices require decentralized, stateless authentication models that allow services to securely interact with each other while enforcing fine-grained access controls. Implementing a robust IAM strategy for microservices involves API-driven identity management, service-to-service authentication, and dynamic authorization mechanisms that ensure security without sacrificing performance or agility.

A fundamental aspect of IAM in microservices is adopting API-driven identity management, where authentication and authorization are handled through secure API calls instead of traditional session management. API-driven IAM enables microservices to authenticate users and services using standardized protocols such as OAuth2, OpenID Connect (OIDC), and JSON Web Tokens (JWTs). These protocols eliminate the need for persistent user sessions by issuing short-lived, stateless access tokens that allow services to validate identities without relying on centralized authentication stores. By leveraging token-based authentication, microservices achieve scalability and resilience while reducing dependency on monolithic IAM systems.

OAuth2 plays a critical role in securing API access within microservices. Instead of requiring each microservice to manage its own authentication logic, OAuth2 delegates authentication to a centralized identity provider (IdP) that issues access tokens upon successful authentication. These tokens contain cryptographic signatures that microservices can verify locally, eliminating the need for repeated authentication requests. OAuth2 grants, such as the client credentials flow and authorization code flow, allow microservices to authenticate users and services securely while enforcing granular access control policies.

Service-to-service authentication is a key requirement in microservices architectures, ensuring that internal services can securely communicate without exposing credentials or relying on static API keys. Unlike traditional IAM, which primarily focuses on user authentication, microservices require strong authentication mechanisms for machine-to-machine (M2M) communication. Mutual TLS (mTLS), OAuth2 client credentials flow, and service mesh-based authentication provide secure, automated identity verification between microservices.

mTLS is one of the most effective methods for securing service-to-service authentication in microservices. By enforcing bidirectional TLS encryption, mTLS ensures that both the client and server authenticate each other before exchanging data. This prevents unauthorized services from interacting with protected APIs, mitigating risks associated with service impersonation and unauthorized API calls.

Service mesh technologies such as Istio and Linkerd provide built-in mTLS enforcement, enabling zero-trust authentication across microservices without requiring direct integration into application code.

OAuth2 client credentials flow is another common approach for securing service-to-service authentication. In this model, a microservice acts as an OAuth2 client, requesting an access token from an IdP using its own credentials. The IdP then issues a token that the microservice can use to authenticate with other services. This approach ensures that only authorized services can access protected APIs while providing a scalable, token-based authentication mechanism that avoids hardcoded credentials.

API gateways play a crucial role in enforcing IAM policies within microservices architectures. As the entry point for external and internal API requests, API gateways act as policy enforcement points (PEPs), validating authentication tokens, enforcing rate limits, and controlling access to backend microservices. API gateways such as Kong, Apigee, AWS API Gateway, and Azure API Management integrate with IAM systems to perform token validation, enforce role-based access control (RBAC) or attribute-based access control (ABAC), and apply API-level security policies.

Fine-grained authorization in microservices IAM requires dynamic access control models that evaluate access requests based on real-time conditions. Traditional role-based access control (RBAC) models become inefficient in microservices environments, as they lack the flexibility needed for dynamic service interactions. Instead, microservices should implement ABAC and Policy-Based Access Control (PBAC), where access decisions consider attributes such as user identity, request context, service permissions, and security policies.

Open Policy Agent (OPA) is a widely adopted policy engine that enables fine-grained authorization in microservices. OPA allows developers to define authorization policies as code using the Rego policy language and enforces these policies at the API gateway, service mesh, or individual microservice level. By decoupling authorization logic from application code, OPA ensures that access control policies remain consistent and centrally managed while enabling real-time policy evaluation.

Workload identity federation is another critical component of microservices IAM, enabling cloud-native workloads to authenticate securely without relying on static credentials. Cloud providers such as AWS, Azure, and Google Cloud offer workload identity federation services that allow microservices to authenticate using dynamic, just-in-time credentials instead of long-lived API keys. AWS IAM Roles for Service Accounts (IRSA), Google Cloud Workload Identity Federation, and Azure Managed Identities eliminate the need for hardcoded credentials while ensuring that service identities are securely managed and automatically rotated.

IAM observability and monitoring are essential for detecting and mitigating identity threats in microservices architectures. Traditional IAM logging mechanisms, which focus on centralized authentication events, are insufficient for tracking service-to-service interactions and API access patterns in distributed environments. Organizations must implement IAM observability frameworks that collect and analyze authentication logs, API calls, and authorization decisions in real time.

Integrating IAM with Security Information and Event Management (SIEM) platforms enhances threat detection by correlating identity-related anomalies with broader security events. User and Entity Behavior Analytics (UEBA) solutions further strengthen IAM security by identifying suspicious access patterns, unauthorized API calls, and privilege escalation attempts within microservices. By continuously monitoring IAM activity across services, organizations can detect and respond to identity-based threats before they impact business operations.

Scalability and performance optimization are critical considerations when architecting IAM for microservices. Traditional IAM systems that rely on centralized authentication databases introduce latency and bottlenecks in high-throughput environments. To mitigate these issues, organizations should implement distributed authentication models that offload token validation to API gateways, service meshes, and edge-based authentication proxies.

Caching authentication tokens at the API gateway or service mesh level reduces the need for repeated authentication requests, improving response times and reducing IAM processing overhead. Using JWTs with short expiration times and refresh tokens ensures that authentication remains efficient while preventing token reuse attacks. Rate limiting and throttling policies further enhance IAM performance by preventing excessive authentication requests from overwhelming identity providers.

By designing an IAM framework that is API-driven, scalable, and optimized for service-to-service authentication, organizations can secure their microservices architectures while maintaining agility and performance. Implementing token-based authentication, dynamic authorization policies, and continuous IAM monitoring ensures that microservices remain protected against identity threats while enabling seamless access management across distributed cloud environments. As enterprises continue adopting microservices, API-driven IAM will remain a foundational component of modern identity security strategies.

IAM in High-Security Environments: Air-Gapped and Classified Network Architectures

Identity and Access Management (IAM) in high-security environments presents unique challenges that go beyond conventional enterprise IAM architectures. Organizations operating in classified networks, defense systems, critical infrastructure, and air-gapped environments must implement stringent identity controls while ensuring operational security and resilience against cyber threats. Unlike traditional IAM systems, which rely on internet-connected authentication services, IAM for high-security environments must function with limited or no external connectivity while enforcing strict identity verification, access segmentation, and continuous monitoring. Architecting IAM for these environments requires a combination of hardware-based authentication, policy-driven access control, and offline identity lifecycle management to prevent unauthorized access and mitigate insider threats.

Air-gapped environments, by design, isolate critical systems from external networks to prevent cyber intrusions and data exfiltration. This physical and logical isolation introduces significant IAM constraints, as traditional cloud-based identity providers and federated authentication mechanisms cannot be directly leveraged. Organizations must implement on-premises IAM solutions that operate entirely within the air-gapped infrastructure while providing robust authentication and authorization capabilities. Directory services such as Active Directory (AD) in disconnected mode, local LDAP instances, and specialized identity vaults must be deployed to store and manage user credentials securely without relying on external synchronization.

Authentication mechanisms in high-security environments must minimize reliance on password-based authentication, as passwords present a significant attack surface due to potential compromise, brute-force attacks, and credential reuse. Strong authentication mechanisms, including Public Key Infrastructure (PKI), smart cards, biometric authentication, and hardware security tokens, must be enforced as mandatory authentication factors. Hardware-based authentication using FIPS 140-2 validated cryptographic modules ensures that credentials remain protected even in classified environments. Implementing certificate-based authentication (CBA) with smart cards or PIV/CAC (Personal Identity Verification / Common Access Card) tokens enhances security by eliminating reliance on passwords while ensuring cryptographic verification of user identities.

Access control in high-security environments must adhere to the principles of least privilege, mandatory access control (MAC), and strict segmentation to prevent unauthorized access to classified resources. Unlike traditional role-based access control (RBAC), which assigns permissions based on predefined job roles, IAM in classified networks often employs Attribute-Based Access Control (ABAC) and Label-Based Access Control (LBAC) to enforce fine-grained access policies. These models evaluate user security clearance levels, data classification labels, and contextual risk factors before granting access to sensitive resources. For example, a user with a "Secret" clearance level should only be able to access documents and systems classified at or below that level, ensuring strict enforcement of data compartmentalization policies.

Identity federation is typically restricted or entirely prohibited in air-gapped and classified network architectures due to the risk of external trust relationships being compromised. Instead of relying on cloud-based identity providers, organizations must deploy isolated identity domains that operate within their own trust boundaries. Offline identity synchronization methods, such as one-way replication from a secure source identity system to classified networks, must be carefully managed to prevent unauthorized data leaks while ensuring accurate identity records. Any synchronization process must be cryptographically signed and validated to prevent tampering or unauthorized identity propagation.

Privileged Access Management (PAM) is a critical component of IAM in high-security environments, ensuring that administrative access is tightly controlled, monitored, and time-bound. Privileged accounts, such as system administrators, security officers, and network operators, pose significant risks if misused or compromised. High-security IAM architectures must enforce just-in-time (JIT) privilege escalation, requiring explicit approval and multi-factor authentication before granting elevated permissions. Implementing one-time-use administrative session credentials, combined with continuous session monitoring and keystroke logging, ensures that privileged activity remains auditable and compliant with security policies.

IAM resilience is a key concern in classified and air-gapped environments, as identity services must remain operational even during cyber incidents, system failures, or physical breaches. Redundant directory services, decentralized authentication mechanisms, and local credential validation must be implemented to ensure continuous access control enforcement. Organizations must also design secure identity recovery mechanisms that do not rely on external identity providers or internet-connected reset workflows. Offline password recovery processes, manual cryptographic key validation, and emergency break-glass access procedures must be rigorously tested to ensure reliability in crisis scenarios.

Insider threats represent one of the most significant risks in high-security IAM architectures. Users with authorized access to classified environments may attempt to misuse their privileges for espionage, sabotage, or data exfiltration. IAM solutions must integrate with real-time User and Entity Behavior Analytics (UEBA) to detect anomalous access patterns, excessive privilege escalation attempts, and unauthorized data access. Security teams must implement zero-trust IAM models that continuously verify user behavior, enforce step-up authentication for high-risk transactions, and revoke access dynamically if suspicious activity is detected.

Auditability and compliance enforcement in high-security IAM require strict identity logging, forensic analysis capabilities, and immutable access records. Every authentication event, privilege escalation request, and system access attempt must be logged in tamper-proof audit trails that cannot be modified or erased by administrators. Logs must be stored in isolated, write-once-read-many (WORM) storage systems that comply with security standards such as NIST 800-53, ISO 27001, and Defense Federal Acquisition Regulation Supplement (DFARS) requirements. Automated log correlation with SIEM (Security Information and Event Management) platforms ensures that security teams receive real-time alerts on identity-related anomalies, enabling rapid incident response and forensic investigations.

High-security environments also demand strict enforcement of identity lifecycle management processes, ensuring that user accounts, machine identities, and privileged credentials are deprovisioned immediately upon termination or role changes. Unlike traditional IAM systems that rely on automated cloud-based identity workflows, classified environments must implement manual and cryptographic identity revocation mechanisms. Secure identity deletion workflows must ensure that all cryptographic credentials, access keys, and identity attributes are securely erased or revoked to prevent unauthorized access post-termination.

Machine identities and workload authentication in classified networks require secure identity provisioning and workload segmentation to prevent lateral movement attacks. Secure enclave technologies, such as Trusted Platform Modules (TPMs) and Hardware Security Modules (HSMs), should be leveraged to store cryptographic identity credentials for non-human entities. Machine-to-machine authentication must be enforced using mutual TLS (mTLS) certificates and policy-based access controls to prevent unauthorized service interactions. Enforcing network segmentation at the identity level ensures that workloads can only communicate with authorized services based on predefined security policies.

By architecting IAM for high-security environments with a focus on air-gapped operations, classified network segmentation, and zero-trust access controls, organizations ensure that identity security remains uncompromised even in the most restrictive operational conditions. The integration of hardware-based authentication, fine-grained access control, privileged session monitoring, and forensic auditability enables enterprises and government agencies to maintain secure identity governance while protecting against insider threats and advanced cyber adversaries. As classified and air-gapped networks continue to evolve, IAM strategies must remain adaptive, ensuring that authentication and authorization mechanisms align with the highest levels of security and compliance requirements.

IAM for Critical Business Applications: ERP, CRM, and SaaS Integration

Identity and Access Management (IAM) is a critical component of securing enterprise resource planning (ERP), customer relationship management (CRM), and Software-as-a-Service (SaaS) applications. These business-critical systems contain sensitive financial data, customer records, intellectual property, and operational workflows that require strict access controls, seamless authentication, and centralized identity governance. Unlike general IT applications, ERP, CRM, and SaaS platforms are deeply integrated into core business processes, making their IAM implementation complex, highly regulated, and subject to stringent security and compliance requirements. Designing an IAM framework that supports secure authentication, fine-grained authorization, and cross-platform identity federation is essential for ensuring that only authorized users, roles, and systems can interact with these applications while minimizing security risks.

ERP systems such as SAP, Oracle ERP Cloud, and Microsoft Dynamics 365 handle financial transactions, procurement, supply chain management, and human resources, making them high-value targets for cyberattacks. Traditional IAM models often struggle to enforce granular access controls in ERP environments due to the complexity of role-based permissions, multi-layered security policies, and custom workflows that vary across organizations. Implementing least privilege access, dynamic authorization policies, and role-based provisioning ensures that ERP users only have the necessary permissions required for their job functions. Enterprises must leverage role mining and entitlement analytics to prevent privilege creep, ensuring that users do not accumulate excessive permissions over time.

CRM applications such as Salesforce, HubSpot, and Oracle CX contain customer profiles, sales pipelines, marketing campaigns, and communication histories that must be protected from unauthorized access and data breaches. CRM platforms often require IAM integration with external identity providers (IdPs) to support federated authentication for employees, partners, and third-party vendors. Implementing Security Assertion Markup Language (SAML) and OpenID Connect (OIDC) for Single Sign-On (SSO) enables seamless access to CRM platforms while enforcing consistent authentication policies across enterprise applications. CRM IAM policies should also incorporate adaptive authentication mechanisms, ensuring that high-risk login attempts trigger additional verification measures, such as multi-factor authentication (MFA) or biometric authentication.

SaaS applications introduce additional IAM complexities, as organizations rely on third-party cloud providers to manage identity authentication, authorization, and access policies. Unlike on-premises ERP and CRM systems, SaaS applications operate in multi-tenant environments where access control policies must align with vendor security requirements. Organizations must integrate SaaS IAM with enterprise IAM platforms, ensuring that user provisioning, deprovisioning, and access reviews are automated and compliant with security policies. Identity federation with SaaS platforms enables centralized authentication, reducing password sprawl and improving user experience. Enterprises must also implement API-based access controls for SaaS integrations, ensuring that service-to-service authentication adheres to OAuth2 and least privilege principles.

IAM for ERP, CRM, and SaaS applications must support federated identity management, enabling secure authentication across multiple systems and organizational boundaries. Federated IAM models allow organizations to establish trust relationships between on-premises identity directories, cloud-based IdPs, and external business partners. By leveraging identity federation protocols such as SAML, OIDC, and OAuth2, enterprises enable users to authenticate once and gain access to multiple business-critical applications without managing separate credentials. Federated IAM also facilitates cross-organization collaboration, allowing partners, contractors, and suppliers to securely access shared resources while maintaining strict identity governance policies.

Fine-grained authorization is essential for IAM implementations in ERP, CRM, and SaaS environments, ensuring that users only access data and functionalities relevant to their job roles. Traditional Role-Based Access Control (RBAC) models often fail to scale efficiently in ERP and CRM applications due to the complexity of permission structures and hierarchical role assignments. Attribute-Based Access Control (ABAC) and Policy-Based Access Control (PBAC) provide more dynamic and scalable alternatives, allowing access decisions to be based on real-time user attributes, transaction context, and security risk levels. For example, ABAC policies can restrict financial transactions in an ERP system based on geographic location, device trust level, and transaction amount, preventing unauthorized actions even if a user has the correct role.

IAM lifecycle management for business-critical applications requires automated provisioning and deprovisioning to ensure that users receive appropriate access levels based on their job functions. Integrating IAM with Human Resources (HR) systems enables real-time identity synchronization, ensuring that employee onboarding, role changes, and terminations trigger automated access modifications. Just-in-Time (JIT) provisioning further enhances security by granting temporary access to ERP, CRM, and SaaS applications only when needed, reducing the risk of standing privileges. Implementing automated role reviews and periodic access certifications ensures that outdated permissions are revoked promptly, preventing unauthorized access due to role misalignment or employee departures.

Privileged Access Management (PAM) is a critical aspect of IAM for ERP and CRM environments, where administrative accounts hold significant control over financial transactions, data exports, and system configurations. Traditional static administrator accounts pose a security risk, as compromised credentials can lead to financial fraud, data breaches, or system sabotage. Implementing just-in-time privileged access escalation, session recording, and multi-factor authentication for administrative actions ensures that ERP and CRM systems remain protected against insider threats and unauthorized privilege escalations. Privileged session monitoring provides real-time visibility into high-risk actions, enabling security teams to detect anomalies and respond to potential security incidents.

IAM security monitoring and anomaly detection play a crucial role in protecting business-critical applications from identity-based attacks. Integrating ERP, CRM, and SaaS IAM logs with Security Information and Event Management (SIEM) platforms enables continuous threat monitoring, detecting unauthorized access attempts, privilege escalations, and suspicious authentication patterns. User and Entity Behavior Analytics (UEBA) further enhances security by identifying deviations from normal user behavior, such as unusual login times, excessive data downloads, or high-risk transactions. Real-time security alerts and automated remediation workflows ensure that identity-related threats are mitigated before they impact business operations.

Compliance and regulatory requirements necessitate stringent IAM controls for ERP, CRM, and SaaS applications, ensuring adherence to industry standards such as GDPR, SOX, HIPAA, and PCI-DSS. IAM policies must enforce data access restrictions, audit logging, and periodic access reviews to demonstrate compliance with security mandates. Implementing fine-grained access policies, automated compliance reporting, and least privilege enforcement ensures that identity management aligns with regulatory expectations while minimizing security risks.

Scalability and performance optimization are critical considerations for IAM in ERP, CRM, and SaaS environments, where thousands of users interact with business-critical applications simultaneously. Implementing distributed authentication, load-balanced IdPs, and token caching strategies ensures that IAM services can handle high transaction volumes without introducing authentication bottlenecks. Edge-based authentication proxies and regional IAM clusters further enhance performance by reducing authentication latency for globally distributed users.

By architecting IAM for critical business applications with a focus on ERP, CRM, and SaaS integration, organizations achieve secure, scalable, and efficient identity management that aligns with business objectives. Implementing federated authentication, fine-grained access control, automated lifecycle management, and continuous security monitoring ensures that enterprise applications remain protected against identity-based threats while enabling seamless access for employees, partners, and customers. As business environments continue evolving, IAM strategies must remain adaptive, ensuring that identity security supports the growing complexity of digital enterprise ecosystems.

Architecting Enterprise IAM for Agile and DevSecOps Environments

Identity and Access Management (IAM) is traditionally associated with rigid security controls, manual provisioning, and compliance-driven access governance. However, as enterprises embrace Agile methodologies and DevSecOps practices, IAM must evolve to support rapid development cycles, automated deployments, and security-as-code approaches. Legacy IAM frameworks, which rely on static role assignments and lengthy approval processes, are often incompatible with modern DevSecOps pipelines that require on-demand access provisioning, dynamic policy enforcement, and seamless integration with CI/CD workflows. Architecting IAM for Agile and DevSecOps environments involves adopting automated identity lifecycle management, just-in-time (JIT) access control, identity federation, and policy-driven security models that align with the speed and flexibility of modern software development.

Traditional IAM approaches introduce friction into Agile workflows by requiring manual intervention for access requests, privilege escalations, and identity verification. In contrast, Agile IAM must be designed for automation, enabling developers, engineers, and security teams to request and receive access dynamically based on predefined policies. Implementing self-service IAM portals, automated access approvals, and identity workflows integrated into DevOps pipelines ensures that IAM becomes an enabler of agility rather than a bottleneck. Role-based access control (RBAC) alone is insufficient in DevSecOps environments due to the complexity of defining static roles for highly dynamic teams. Instead, organizations should implement Attribute-Based Access Control (ABAC) and Policy-Based Access Control (PBAC) to allow access decisions based on real-time attributes such as project ownership, environment type, security risk, and user context.

IAM automation plays a crucial role in Agile and DevSecOps environments, reducing the dependency on manual access provisioning and ensuring that identities are managed programmatically. Infrastructure-as-Code (IaC) principles should extend to IAM configurations, allowing access policies, role definitions, and identity workflows to be codified and version-controlled alongside application infrastructure. Using tools such as Terraform, AWS CloudFormation, and Azure Bicep, enterprises can define IAM policies as code, ensuring that identity configurations are consistently deployed across development, testing, and production environments. IAM-as-Code ensures that security policies remain immutable, auditable, and easily replicated across multiple cloud and on-premises environments.

Just-in-Time (JIT) access control is essential for reducing standing privileges in DevSecOps environments, where developers and engineers frequently require temporary elevated access to deploy, troubleshoot, or modify infrastructure components. Instead of granting persistent administrative access, organizations should implement ephemeral privilege escalation mechanisms that provide short-lived credentials or time-restricted permissions based on workload requirements. Temporary access can be granted through automated approval workflows, integrating with chat-based tools such as Slack, Microsoft Teams, or Jira for real-time access provisioning and revocation. Implementing Privileged Access Management (PAM) with JIT access ensures that administrative privileges are granted only when necessary and revoked automatically after the task is completed, minimizing the risk of credential misuse or insider threats.

Identity federation is a critical component of IAM in Agile and DevSecOps environments, enabling seamless authentication and authorization across multiple cloud platforms, SaaS applications, and collaboration tools. By leveraging OpenID Connect (OIDC), Security Assertion Markup Language (SAML), and OAuth2, enterprises can implement Single Sign-On (SSO) across developer platforms, cloud providers, and CI/CD pipelines, reducing the complexity of managing separate credentials for each system. Identity federation allows DevSecOps teams to authenticate using enterprise identity providers (IdPs) while enforcing centralized security policies, access logging, and risk-based authentication.

DevSecOps environments require secure service-to-service authentication, ensuring that automated workloads, APIs, and infrastructure components interact securely without relying on hardcoded credentials. Traditional IAM models often fail to accommodate the dynamic nature of microservices, containers, and serverless computing, where applications scale dynamically and require machine identities that rotate frequently. Implementing workload identity federation using cloud-native IAM services such as AWS IAM Roles for Service Accounts (IRSA), Google Workload Identity Federation, and Azure Managed Identities ensures that services authenticate securely using ephemeral credentials rather than static API keys. Mutual TLS (mTLS) authentication, OAuth2 client credentials flow, and SPIFFE-based workload identity frameworks further strengthen service authentication in DevSecOps architectures.

Continuous authorization and risk-based access control enhance security in Agile IAM frameworks by dynamically evaluating access decisions throughout the software development lifecycle. Instead of static role assignments, IAM policies should enforce real-time risk assessments that adjust access permissions based on contextual factors such as device security posture, geolocation, behavioral anomalies, and workload sensitivity. Continuous authorization enables security teams to implement adaptive access policies that enforce step-up authentication for high-risk actions, reducing the likelihood of unauthorized privilege escalation.

IAM observability and monitoring must be deeply integrated into DevSecOps workflows, providing real-time visibility into authentication attempts, access patterns, and potential security violations. By aggregating IAM logs with Security Information and Event Management (SIEM) platforms such as Splunk, Azure Sentinel, or Google Chronicle, organizations can detect suspicious access behaviors, automate incident response workflows, and enforce compliance reporting. User and Entity Behavior Analytics (UEBA) further strengthens security by identifying deviations from normal access patterns, flagging potential account takeovers, excessive privilege escalations, or anomalous API calls.

Compliance automation is essential for IAM in DevSecOps, ensuring that identity governance aligns with regulatory requirements without disrupting Agile workflows. Many security frameworks, including SOC 2, GDPR, HIPAA, and PCI-DSS, mandate strict access control policies, identity auditing, and privilege management. Implementing Compliance-as-Code automates IAM compliance enforcement by continuously validating access policies against regulatory baselines. DevSecOps teams can integrate compliance validation into CI/CD pipelines, automatically checking IAM configurations for misconfigurations, excessive privileges, and policy violations before deploying changes to production environments.

IAM resilience in Agile environments requires high availability and fault-tolerant authentication mechanisms to prevent disruptions to development and deployment workflows. Distributed IAM architectures that leverage multiple identity providers, redundant authentication nodes, and regional failover mechanisms ensure that authentication services remain operational even during outages. Edge-based authentication caching and API token acceleration techniques reduce authentication latency for globally distributed DevSecOps teams, ensuring a seamless developer experience while maintaining security controls.

DevSecOps IAM strategies must also incorporate self-service identity management capabilities, enabling developers and engineers to manage access requests, role assignments, and authentication settings without relying on IT administrators. Implementing IAM self-service portals, automated role approvals, and delegated identity governance streamlines access management while maintaining security oversight. Developers should have the ability to request permissions dynamically based on pre-approved security policies, reducing access delays while ensuring that IAM controls remain aligned with security best practices.

By architecting IAM for Agile and DevSecOps environments with automation, federated identity, just-in-time access, continuous authorization, and compliance-as-code, organizations can achieve security without compromising agility. Aligning IAM with DevSecOps principles ensures that security becomes an integrated component of the development lifecycle rather than an obstacle to innovation. As enterprises continue to adopt cloud-native development, microservices, and continuous deployment models, IAM strategies must evolve to support the speed, scale, and security requirements of modern software engineering.

IAM Infrastructure as Code: Automating IAM Deployments with Terraform and Kubernetes

Identity and Access Management (IAM) has traditionally been managed as a static, manual process, requiring administrators to configure roles, permissions, and policies through web-based consoles or command-line tools. However, as enterprises adopt cloud-native architectures and DevSecOps methodologies, IAM must evolve to align with automated, scalable, and repeatable deployment models. Infrastructure as Code (IaC) enables organizations to define IAM configurations as machine-readable code, ensuring that identity policies, role assignments, and authentication mechanisms can be provisioned, version-controlled, and deployed consistently across environments. By leveraging Terraform and Kubernetes for IAM automation, enterprises achieve greater security, operational efficiency, and compliance while reducing the risk of misconfigurations and privilege escalation.

Terraform is one of the most widely used IaC tools for automating IAM deployments across cloud platforms. Unlike traditional IAM management approaches that require manual role creation and policy assignment, Terraform enables security teams to codify IAM policies in declarative configurations. These configurations define IAM roles, policies, identity providers, and access control lists (ACLs) as code, allowing organizations to maintain IAM configurations in version-controlled repositories. Using Terraform, enterprises can enforce least privilege access by programmatically defining IAM policies that align with security best practices and regulatory requirements.

By adopting Terraform for IAM, security teams eliminate inconsistencies in IAM configurations across multiple cloud environments. Instead of manually configuring IAM roles in AWS, Azure, and Google Cloud, organizations can use Terraform modules to define standardized IAM templates that apply consistent security policies across all platforms. Terraform's ability to manage IAM resources across cloud providers ensures that identity governance remains uniform, reducing the risk of excessive privileges, orphaned accounts, and misconfigured access controls.

IAM policy automation with Terraform allows organizations to enforce security-by-design principles by integrating IAM provisioning into CI/CD pipelines. Instead of relying on ad hoc IAM updates, security teams can define IAM configurations in Terraform files and deploy them as part of automated infrastructure deployments. This ensures that IAM policies are reviewed, tested, and approved before being applied to production environments. By integrating Terraform IAM modules with Git repositories and code review workflows, organizations enhance identity governance by enforcing change control, role-based approvals, and auditability for IAM modifications.

Role-based access control (RBAC) and attribute-based access control (ABAC) policies can be defined and managed using Terraform, ensuring that access permissions remain aligned with security policies. For example, organizations can create Terraform modules that define

IAM roles for developers, administrators, and security analysts, assigning only the minimum necessary permissions for each role. Terraform also enables organizations to dynamically assign IAM permissions based on infrastructure attributes, ensuring that access control policies adapt to changing business requirements.

Kubernetes introduces additional IAM challenges, as workloads running in Kubernetes clusters require secure authentication and authorization mechanisms. Kubernetes-native IAM solutions, such as Kubernetes Role-Based Access Control (RBAC) and OpenID Connect (OIDC) authentication, allow organizations to define granular access policies for Kubernetes resources. Automating Kubernetes IAM with Terraform enables enterprises to manage Kubernetes role bindings, service account permissions, and API access controls as code, ensuring that identity policies are applied consistently across clusters.

Terraform can be used to automate Kubernetes IAM by defining Kubernetes role bindings and service accounts in Terraform configurations. Instead of manually assigning Kubernetes RBAC policies through the Kubernetes API, organizations can use Terraform to create and apply IAM policies programmatically. This approach ensures that Kubernetes IAM policies remain consistent across clusters, reducing the risk of privilege misconfigurations and unauthorized access to Kubernetes workloads.

Workload identity federation in Kubernetes is essential for securing service-to-service authentication without relying on static API keys. Kubernetes workloads must authenticate with external cloud services, databases, and APIs using secure identity mechanisms. By integrating Kubernetes IAM with cloud-native identity providers, such as AWS IAM Roles for Service Accounts (IRSA), Google Workload Identity Federation, and Azure Managed Identities, organizations enable workloads to obtain short-lived, just-in-time credentials without exposing long-lived secrets. Terraform simplifies workload identity federation by automating the provisioning of federated IAM roles and policies, ensuring that Kubernetes workloads authenticate securely across multi-cloud environments.

IAM compliance automation is another key benefit of adopting Terraform for IAM management. Many regulatory frameworks, such as

GDPR, PCI-DSS, and HIPAA, mandate strict IAM controls, including access logging, privilege reviews, and role segregation. Terraform allows security teams to define compliance-driven IAM policies as code, ensuring that identity configurations remain aligned with regulatory requirements. By integrating Terraform with policy-as-code frameworks, such as Open Policy Agent (OPA) and HashiCorp Sentinel, organizations can enforce IAM compliance rules dynamically, preventing misconfigurations before they are deployed.

IAM observability and auditing are critical for maintaining security visibility in cloud-native environments. Terraform enables organizations to configure IAM logging and monitoring settings as code, ensuring that authentication logs, access control decisions, and IAM policy changes are automatically collected and analyzed. By defining IAM logging configurations in Terraform, organizations can ensure that IAM events are forwarded to SIEM platforms, such as Splunk, Azure Sentinel, or Google Chronicle, for real-time identity threat detection.

IAM resilience and disaster recovery can also be automated using Terraform. In traditional IAM deployments, identity configurations must be manually recreated in the event of a system failure, leading to potential downtime and security gaps. Terraform allows organizations to define IAM infrastructure snapshots that can be redeployed automatically, ensuring that identity services remain operational even in disaster scenarios. By storing IAM configurations in version-controlled repositories, enterprises can roll back to previous IAM states in the event of unauthorized changes or security incidents.

Integrating IAM automation with DevSecOps pipelines ensures that identity security remains an integral part of software development and deployment workflows. Terraform IAM modules can be embedded in CI/CD pipelines, automatically provisioning IAM roles and access policies for new applications, environments, and services. By enforcing IAM policies at the infrastructure level, organizations prevent unauthorized access from the earliest stages of application deployment, ensuring that security controls remain embedded within development workflows.

IAM policy validation with Terraform ensures that access permissions are reviewed before deployment, preventing privilege escalation risks and policy misconfigurations. Organizations can use static IAM analysis tools, such as IAM Access Analyzer and tfsec, to validate Terraform IAM configurations against security best practices. Automated IAM policy linting and compliance validation prevent overly permissive IAM policies from being deployed, ensuring that access control remains tightly managed.

By leveraging Terraform and Kubernetes for IAM automation, organizations achieve scalable, repeatable, and secure IAM deployments that align with cloud-native architectures and DevSecOps principles. Automating IAM with infrastructure as code ensures that identity policies remain consistent, auditable, and dynamically enforceable across cloud and Kubernetes environments. As IAM complexity continues to grow in multi-cloud and hybrid infrastructures, adopting Terraform and Kubernetes IAM automation provides enterprises with the agility and security needed to manage identity at scale.

IAM and Quantum Security: Future-Proofing Identity Against Post-Quantum Threats

The rise of quantum computing presents a transformative shift in cybersecurity, with significant implications for Identity and Access Management (IAM). While quantum computing promises advancements in fields such as cryptography, artificial intelligence, and materials science, it also threatens the security foundations that IAM systems rely on. Classical cryptographic methods used for authentication, encryption, and digital signatures—such as RSA, ECC, and Diffie-Hellman—are vulnerable to quantum attacks. Once large-scale quantum computers become viable, adversaries will be able to break these cryptographic schemes, rendering current IAM systems obsolete. Future-proofing IAM against post-quantum threats requires a strategic transition to quantum-resistant cryptographic algorithms, secure key management, and adaptive authentication mechanisms that ensure long-term security resilience.

Quantum threats primarily stem from Shor's algorithm, which enables quantum computers to efficiently factor large integers and compute discrete logarithms—fundamentally breaking RSA, ECC, and Diffie-Hellman encryption. These cryptographic methods underpin IAM processes, including secure authentication, digital certificates, secure key exchange, and federated identity protocols such as SAML, OAuth2, and OpenID Connect (OIDC). If these encryption schemes are compromised, attackers could decrypt stored authentication data, forge digital signatures, and impersonate users across IAM ecosystems. Organizations must prepare for a transition to post-quantum cryptography (PQC) to ensure that identity security remains intact against future quantum-capable adversaries.

The National Institute of Standards and Technology (NIST) has been leading efforts to standardize post-quantum cryptographic algorithms that resist quantum attacks. These algorithms include lattice-based, hash-based, multivariate polynomial, and code-based cryptographic schemes, which are designed to replace existing public-key encryption and signature algorithms. IAM architects must integrate these quantum-safe algorithms into authentication protocols, identity federation mechanisms, and certificate management systems to mitigate the risks posed by quantum computing. The transition to PQC is a complex, multi-phase process that requires evaluating IAM dependencies on vulnerable cryptographic schemes and replacing them with quantum-resistant alternatives.

IAM systems must undergo cryptographic agility, enabling seamless upgrades to post-quantum encryption without disrupting authentication workflows. Cryptographic agility allows IAM platforms to support multiple cryptographic algorithms simultaneously, ensuring compatibility with existing authentication mechanisms while enabling a gradual transition to PQC. Organizations should adopt hybrid encryption models that combine classical cryptographic schemes with quantum-resistant algorithms, ensuring backward compatibility while preparing for a quantum-secure future. Hybrid authentication mechanisms, which use both classical and post-quantum digital signatures, provide a transitional approach that maintains security even as quantum threats evolve.

Key management is a critical component of quantum-resistant IAM. Current key exchange mechanisms, such as TLS key negotiation and OAuth2 token signing, rely on cryptographic primitives that will be broken by quantum computing. Organizations must implement post-quantum key exchange protocols, such as lattice-based key encapsulation mechanisms (KEMs), to ensure that authentication tokens and encrypted credentials remain secure against quantum decryption attacks. Secure key rotation policies must be enforced to transition existing cryptographic keys to quantum-resistant equivalents, ensuring that IAM systems do not retain legacy encryption methods that may become vulnerable over time.

Federated IAM models, including SAML, OIDC, and OAuth2, must be adapted to support quantum-safe authentication mechanisms. Many identity federation protocols rely on asymmetric cryptographic signatures for token verification and trust establishment between identity providers (IdPs) and service providers (SPs). Quantum-resistant signature schemes, such as hash-based and lattice-based signatures, must replace RSA and ECC-based digital signatures in identity assertions, OAuth2 access tokens, and authentication request signing. Organizations must evaluate identity federation dependencies on quantum-vulnerable cryptographic schemes and upgrade identity provider infrastructures to support post-quantum authentication.

Biometric authentication and passwordless authentication mechanisms must also be evaluated for quantum security. While biometric authentication does not rely on public-key encryption directly, many biometric systems use cryptographic hash functions and digital signatures for template protection and authentication integrity. Transitioning biometric IAM systems to quantum-resistant cryptographic primitives ensures that biometric data remains secure against emerging quantum threats. Similarly, passwordless authentication solutions, including FIDO2 and WebAuthn, must adopt post-quantum cryptographic algorithms to maintain long-term security resilience.

IAM resilience against quantum threats also requires enhanced identity monitoring, threat intelligence, and continuous authentication mechanisms. Security teams must proactively monitor for cryptographic vulnerabilities, ensuring that IAM systems remain resistant to quantum decryption attacks. Integrating IAM with Security Information and Event Management (SIEM) platforms provides real-time visibility into identity threats, enabling organizations to detect quantum-related attack attempts and unauthorized decryption activities. Continuous authentication models that dynamically reassess authentication trust throughout a user session enhance security by mitigating risks associated with compromised quantum-vulnerable credentials.

The transition to quantum-safe IAM must be incorporated into enterprise security roadmaps, ensuring that IAM policies, identity governance frameworks, and compliance mandates align with post-quantum security requirements. Regulatory bodies, including the European Union Agency for Cybersecurity (ENISA) and the U.S. National Security Agency (NSA), are expected to mandate quantum-resistant cryptographic adoption for IAM systems handling sensitive government, financial, and healthcare data. Enterprises operating in regulated industries must develop quantum migration strategies, ensuring that IAM infrastructures comply with emerging post-quantum security standards.

Hybrid cloud and multi-cloud IAM architectures require special consideration in the context of quantum security. Many cloud service providers (CSPs) rely on classical encryption methods to secure IAM credentials, identity federation mechanisms, and API authentication workflows. Organizations using cloud-native IAM solutions must work with CSPs to ensure that post-quantum cryptographic support is integrated into IAM services. Secure workload identity management, service-to-service authentication, and API gateway authentication must adopt quantum-resistant key exchange mechanisms to prevent quantum-enabled eavesdropping attacks.

Machine identities and IoT device authentication introduce additional challenges in quantum-safe IAM. Many IoT devices rely on lightweight cryptographic schemes that will be vulnerable to quantum attacks. Transitioning IoT IAM frameworks to support post-quantum cryptography requires optimizing authentication protocols to work within the processing and power constraints of embedded systems. Lightweight post-quantum cryptographic algorithms, such as NTRUEncrypt and XMSS-based signatures, must be integrated into IoT IAM solutions to ensure secure device authentication and encrypted communication in quantum-threatened environments.

As organizations prepare for a quantum-secure IAM future, security teams must conduct cryptographic inventory assessments to identify IAM components that rely on quantum-vulnerable algorithms. Developing phased migration plans, testing quantum-resistant IAM deployments, and adopting cryptographic agility strategies ensure that IAM infrastructures remain secure against emerging threats. Quantum-resistant IAM is not an immediate necessity, but enterprises that delay preparation risk being unprepared when quantum computing reaches practical cryptographic-breaking capabilities.

Future-proofing IAM against post-quantum threats requires a proactive approach, integrating cryptographic agility, quantum-resistant encryption, and identity governance frameworks that support evolving security standards. As quantum computing advances, organizations must ensure that IAM systems are prepared to withstand the challenges of a post-quantum security landscape, protecting authentication mechanisms, identity federation models, and machine-to-machine authentication against next-generation cyber threats. By adopting a strategic transition plan, enterprises can safeguard IAM infrastructures, ensuring that identity security remains resilient in an era of quantum computing advancements.

IAM Ecosystem Integration: Architecting for IAM Interoperability and API Extensions

Identity and Access Management (IAM) ecosystems are becoming increasingly complex as enterprises integrate multiple identity providers, cloud platforms, SaaS applications, and legacy authentication systems. Ensuring interoperability across diverse IAM components is critical to maintaining seamless authentication, consistent authorization policies, and secure identity governance. Traditional IAM solutions often struggle with integration challenges due to proprietary protocols, inconsistent API designs, and fragmented access control mechanisms. Architecting IAM for interoperability requires designing extensible identity frameworks that support open standards, API-driven authentication, and dynamic identity federation, ensuring that IAM can adapt to evolving business and security requirements.

Interoperability in IAM begins with adopting industry-standard authentication and authorization protocols. Security Assertion Markup Language (SAML), OpenID Connect (OIDC), and OAuth2 serve as foundational standards for federated authentication, enabling identity providers (IdPs) and service providers (SPs) to exchange authentication and authorization information securely. SAML remains widely used in enterprise IAM for Single Sign-On (SSO) between corporate applications and SaaS platforms, while OIDC and OAuth2 provide modern, API-driven authentication mechanisms for web and mobile applications. Ensuring that IAM components support these protocols enables seamless integration across heterogeneous identity environments, reducing authentication silos and minimizing the need for proprietary connectors.

API-driven IAM integration is essential for enabling scalable and flexible identity workflows. Traditional IAM solutions often rely on rigid user provisioning and access management processes that require manual intervention or batch synchronization. Modern IAM architectures must expose well-defined RESTful APIs that allow applications, DevSecOps pipelines, and third-party identity services to programmatically manage identities, access tokens, and authorization policies. API-driven IAM allows enterprises to automate identity lifecycle management, implement real-time access control decisions, and dynamically enforce authentication policies based on contextual risk factors.

Extending IAM through API integrations ensures that identity services can accommodate evolving business needs and security requirements. Enterprises often require custom IAM extensions for unique authentication flows, identity federation scenarios, and cross-domain access control. IAM platforms should provide API extension capabilities that allow developers to create custom authentication adapters, policy evaluation engines, and attribute enrichment services. For example, a financial institution may need to integrate IAM with fraud detection systems that evaluate transaction risk before granting authorization, requiring real-time API calls to external risk engines. By designing IAM ecosystems with extensible APIs, organizations can build modular identity frameworks that evolve alongside digital transformation initiatives.

Identity federation is a key component of IAM interoperability, enabling organizations to establish trust relationships between multiple identity domains. As enterprises adopt hybrid and multi-cloud architectures, federated IAM ensures that users can authenticate across cloud providers, on-premises directories, and third-party SaaS applications without maintaining separate credentials. Federation protocols such as SAML and OIDC allow IAM systems to delegate authentication to external identity providers while enforcing centralized access policies. Federated IAM also enables organizations to integrate with partner ecosystems, allowing business-to-business (B2B) and business-to-consumer (B2C) authentication without duplicating identity records across domains.

Microservices-based IAM architectures further enhance interoperability by decoupling authentication and authorization services from application logic. Unlike monolithic IAM systems that tightly couple identity management with specific applications, microservices IAM exposes identity functions as independent services that can be consumed by multiple applications. Implementing IAM as a service mesh component, using tools like Istio or Linkerd, allows authentication and authorization to be enforced at the network layer, ensuring consistent identity policies across distributed environments. API gateways play a critical role in IAM integration by acting as policy enforcement points (PEPs), validating access tokens, managing rate limits, and enforcing attribute-based access control (ABAC) policies at the API level.

IAM orchestration enables seamless user provisioning and access synchronization across integrated systems. Organizations must implement IAM orchestration platforms that synchronize identity attributes, role assignments, and access policies between cloud and on-premises IAM systems. SCIM (System for Cross-domain Identity Management) is a widely adopted protocol for automated user provisioning, enabling IAM platforms to create, update, and delete user accounts across multiple SaaS applications in real time. By leveraging SCIM APIs, enterprises can ensure that identity records remain consistent across business applications, reducing administrative overhead and mitigating the risk of orphaned accounts.

API security is a critical consideration in IAM ecosystem integration, as exposing IAM services through APIs introduces potential attack vectors. API authentication must enforce strong security mechanisms, including OAuth2 client credentials flow, mutual TLS (mTLS), and API key management. IAM APIs must be protected against common API threats, such as token replay attacks, excessive privilege escalation, and API abuse. Implementing rate limiting, request signing, and API threat analytics ensures that IAM APIs remain secure while maintaining high availability for integrated applications.

IAM logging and monitoring enhance interoperability by providing real-time insights into authentication events, access requests, and identity-related security incidents. Integrating IAM logs with Security Information and Event Management (SIEM) platforms allows organizations to correlate identity activities with broader security threats, detecting anomalies such as excessive failed login attempts, unusual privilege escalations, and API abuse patterns. Centralized IAM logging ensures that identity governance policies remain auditable, enabling compliance with security standards such as GDPR, HIPAA, and SOC 2.

IAM governance frameworks must be designed to support cross-platform identity management while enforcing consistent access control policies. Organizations should adopt Identity Governance and Administration (IGA) solutions that provide automated role management, periodic access reviews, and compliance-driven access certification processes. IAM governance must extend beyond human identities to include machine identities, API credentials, and workload authentication mechanisms, ensuring that all identity interactions remain secure and policy-compliant.

Multi-cloud IAM strategies require interoperability across cloud-native identity providers, including AWS IAM, Azure Active Directory (Azure AD), and Google Cloud IAM. Each cloud provider implements its own IAM framework, creating challenges for organizations that require unified access control policies across multi-cloud deployments. Implementing a cloud-agnostic IAM layer that abstracts identity management from cloud-specific IAM services ensures that enterprises can enforce consistent security policies across cloud environments. Federated authentication, workload identity federation, and cross-cloud policy synchronization are essential components of a multi-cloud IAM integration strategy.

IAM modernization efforts must prioritize interoperability by adopting open standards, API-driven automation, and flexible identity federation models. Legacy IAM systems that rely on static role assignments and manual identity synchronization must be replaced with dynamic, policy-driven IAM frameworks that support real-time access control decisions. Organizations should leverage IAM platforms that provide built-in API extensibility, allowing security teams to integrate identity services with custom authentication providers, threat intelligence platforms, and adaptive risk engines.

By architecting IAM ecosystems for interoperability and API extensions, organizations achieve scalable, resilient, and future-proof identity management frameworks. Ensuring that IAM components integrate seamlessly across cloud, SaaS, and on-premises environments enhances security, improves user experience, and streamlines identity governance. As digital transformation accelerates, enterprises must build IAM ecosystems that prioritize extensibility, automation, and interoperability, ensuring that identity security remains adaptive to evolving business and technology landscapes.

Securing Machine Learning and AI Pipelines with IAM Controls

As organizations increasingly rely on artificial intelligence (AI) and machine learning (ML) to drive business decisions, the security of AI pipelines becomes a critical concern. AI models require vast amounts of data, computational resources, and automation, making them highly attractive targets for cyber threats, insider attacks, and data breaches. Identity and Access Management (IAM) plays a crucial role in securing ML and AI workflows by enforcing strict authentication, authorization, and identity governance controls across the AI development lifecycle. Implementing IAM controls for AI pipelines ensures that data integrity, model confidentiality, and computational environments remain protected from unauthorized access, privilege escalation, and adversarial manipulation.

AI pipelines typically involve multiple stages, including data ingestion, preprocessing, model training, validation, deployment, and monitoring. Each stage requires secure access controls to prevent unauthorized data exposure, tampering, or misuse of computing resources. IAM must be integrated into the entire AI workflow to ensure that only authorized users, services, and workloads can interact with AI datasets, model artifacts, and inference endpoints. Unlike traditional software development, ML workflows introduce unique security challenges, such as securing sensitive training datasets, controlling access to pre-trained models, and enforcing trust in model inference results.

Data security is one of the most critical IAM concerns in AI pipelines, as training datasets often contain personally identifiable information (PII), financial records, proprietary business data, or classified intelligence. Organizations must implement role-based access control (RBAC) and attribute-based access control (ABAC) to enforce fine-grained permissions on dataset access. Data scientists, ML engineers, and AI auditors should only be granted the minimum level of access necessary to perform their tasks. IAM policies should restrict unauthorized users and workloads from accessing raw datasets, ensuring that sensitive training data remains protected from unauthorized exposure or theft.

IAM solutions must also enforce encryption policies for AI datasets at rest and in transit. Cloud-based AI platforms, such as AWS SageMaker, Azure Machine Learning, and Google Vertex AI, provide IAM-integrated encryption mechanisms that allow organizations to secure training datasets using customer-managed keys. Implementing IAM policies that enforce encryption at the data storage layer prevents unauthorized entities from extracting sensitive training data, even if storage credentials are compromised. Secure data tokenization and anonymization further enhance AI pipeline security by replacing sensitive data fields with pseudonymous identifiers before they are used in training models.

Model integrity is another major security concern in AI pipelines, as adversarial attacks can manipulate training data or inject backdoors into AI models. IAM controls must restrict access to model training environments, ensuring that only trusted data sources and authorized users can modify model parameters. Organizations should implement IAM policies that verify the identity of ML engineers before granting permission to update training datasets, hyperparameters, or model architectures. Version control systems, such as Git, must be integrated with IAM to track model changes and enforce access restrictions on model modifications.

AI model artifacts, including trained weights, feature extractors, and inference engines, must be stored securely in access-controlled model repositories. IAM should enforce strict access policies on AI model storage locations, ensuring that only authorized ML pipelines and deployment services can retrieve models for inference. Organizations should adopt AI-specific secret management solutions to protect model credentials, API keys, and container registry authentication tokens. Secure model registries, such as AWS SageMaker Model Registry or Azure ML Model Management, allow enterprises to apply IAM policies that restrict model access based on project ownership, risk classification, and regulatory compliance requirements.

Inference security is a critical aspect of AI IAM, as deployed models can be exploited through adversarial inputs, unauthorized API access, or API abuse. IAM policies must control access to inference endpoints, ensuring that only verified users and trusted applications can interact with AI decision-making systems. Organizations should implement OAuth2 authentication and API gateway enforcement to restrict public access to AI inference APIs, preventing unauthorized model queries and inference manipulation attempts. Rate limiting and anomaly detection further enhance AI security by blocking excessive requests that could indicate a model extraction or poisoning attack.

IAM governance for AI pipelines must extend beyond human identity management to include machine identities, workload authentication, and service-to-service authorization. AI models often interact with cloud computing resources, distributed data storage, and external APIs, requiring secure workload authentication mechanisms. Machine identities should be managed through IAM roles, workload identity federation, and mutual TLS (mTLS) to ensure that AI components authenticate securely without relying on hardcoded credentials. IAM policies should enforce just-in-time (JIT) access for AI workloads, granting temporary access tokens for specific ML tasks and revoking permissions once computations are completed.

Auditing and monitoring are essential components of AI IAM security, providing real-time visibility into identity-related activities across the AI pipeline. Organizations must integrate IAM logs with Security Information and Event Management (SIEM) platforms to detect anomalies, unauthorized access attempts, and suspicious model modifications. User and Entity Behavior Analytics (UEBA) enhances AI IAM security by identifying deviations in access patterns, such as an AI researcher suddenly attempting to download large datasets or modify inference rules without prior approval. Continuous IAM monitoring ensures that AI pipelines remain protected against privilege misuse, insider threats, and automated attacks.

Regulatory compliance and IAM governance for AI pipelines are increasingly important as governments and industry regulators introduce AI-specific security mandates. Regulations such as GDPR, CCPA, and emerging AI governance frameworks require organizations to enforce strict data access policies, audit AI decision-making, and prevent unauthorized AI model modifications. IAM policies must align with compliance requirements by implementing access reviews, data classification enforcement, and AI model risk assessments. Periodic access reviews should be conducted to ensure that AI researchers, developers, and external contractors do not retain unnecessary access to AI datasets and models.

Zero Trust IAM principles should be integrated into AI pipeline security, ensuring continuous identity verification and least privilege enforcement at every stage of the AI lifecycle. Instead of assuming implicit trust for authenticated users, Zero Trust IAM enforces adaptive authentication policies based on contextual risk signals. AI developers working from untrusted networks should be required to pass additional authentication factors, such as biometric verification or hardware security tokens, before accessing training datasets or AI model repositories. By continuously evaluating risk levels, Zero Trust IAM minimizes unauthorized AI data access and prevents adversarial manipulation of ML models.

IAM automation plays a crucial role in securing AI pipelines, reducing manual identity provisioning overhead and ensuring consistent enforcement of access policies. Infrastructure-as-Code (IaC) frameworks, such as Terraform and Kubernetes RBAC, enable organizations to define AI IAM policies as code, automating identity configurations across cloud-based AI platforms. IAM-as-Code ensures that AI identity policies are version-controlled, auditable, and easily deployable across multiple environments. Automating IAM for AI workloads enhances scalability while maintaining security best practices.

By securing AI pipelines with IAM controls, organizations ensure that ML models, training datasets, and inference endpoints remain protected from unauthorized access, adversarial attacks, and regulatory non-compliance. Implementing robust authentication, authorization, encryption, and monitoring mechanisms allows enterprises to develop AI applications with confidence, ensuring that identity security remains a foundational component of AI-driven decision-making. As AI continues to evolve, IAM strategies must adapt to safeguard AI ecosystems against emerging threats, ensuring that machine learning remains a secure and trustworthy technology.

IAM Disaster Recovery and Business Continuity Planning for Global Organizations

Identity and Access Management (IAM) is a mission-critical component of enterprise security, ensuring that users, applications, and machines can authenticate and access resources securely. Any disruption to IAM systems can have severe consequences, leading to operational downtime, security vulnerabilities, compliance failures, and financial losses. Global organizations must develop comprehensive IAM disaster recovery (DR) and business continuity planning (BCP) strategies to ensure that authentication, authorization, and identity governance functions remain resilient in the face of cyberattacks, infrastructure failures, and other catastrophic events. IAM must be architected with high availability, failover mechanisms, redundancy, and automated recovery processes to maintain business operations and protect digital identities across global environments.

IAM disaster recovery planning begins with identifying critical identity services that must be prioritized for resilience. Core IAM components include authentication services, identity directories, access control policies, Single Sign-On (SSO) systems, privileged access management (PAM) solutions, multi-factor authentication (MFA), and identity governance platforms. Any failure in these components can lock users out of critical applications, disrupt automated workflows, and prevent security teams from enforcing compliance policies. Organizations must conduct a risk assessment to evaluate IAM dependencies, determine potential failure points, and classify identity services based on their impact on business continuity.

High availability (HA) architectures play a crucial role in IAM resilience by ensuring that identity services remain operational during system failures, network outages, or cloud service disruptions. Organizations should implement active-active IAM deployments across multiple geographic regions to distribute authentication traffic and prevent single points of failure. Redundant identity providers, load-balanced authentication endpoints, and replicated identity stores ensure that IAM services can handle failover scenarios without degrading performance. By leveraging cloud-native IAM solutions with multi-region redundancy, organizations can maintain continuous authentication and authorization capabilities even if a primary IAM instance becomes unavailable.

Replication and backup strategies are essential for ensuring IAM data integrity in disaster recovery scenarios. Identity directories, including Active Directory (AD), LDAP-based identity stores, and cloud identity providers, must be replicated in real-time to secondary environments to prevent identity loss or corruption. Organizations should implement multi-master replication for IAM databases, ensuring that identity records, access control lists, and authentication logs are synchronized across disaster recovery sites. Automated IAM backups must be performed at regular intervals, and recovery testing should be conducted to verify that identity data can be restored quickly in the event of a failure.

IAM disaster recovery planning must also account for cloud-based identity federation and third-party authentication dependencies. Many global organizations rely on federated identity providers (IdPs) such as Azure AD, Okta, Ping Identity, and Google Cloud Identity for cross-domain authentication. A disruption to a cloud IdP can prevent users from accessing SaaS applications, cloud workloads, and external business platforms. To mitigate this risk, organizations should implement secondary identity federation mechanisms, such as backup SAML or OpenID Connect (OIDC) providers, that can take over authentication duties if the primary IdP becomes unavailable. Hybrid IAM architectures that combine on-premises and cloud-based identity management ensure resilience by providing alternative authentication paths during cloud outages.

Privileged access management (PAM) resilience is a critical aspect of IAM disaster recovery, as privileged accounts control administrative access to enterprise infrastructure, cloud environments, and security systems. Organizations must implement just-in-time (JIT) privilege escalation, ephemeral administrative credentials, and PAM vault replication to ensure that privileged users can securely access critical systems even during IAM disruptions. Backup privileged access workflows should be predefined, allowing emergency administrative sessions to be initiated using break-glass accounts with strict audit logging and real-time monitoring.

Multi-factor authentication (MFA) availability must be factored into IAM disaster recovery planning, as MFA outages can prevent legitimate users from accessing enterprise systems. Organizations should implement redundant MFA providers, ensuring that authentication methods such as hardware tokens, biometric authentication, and one-time passcodes (OTP) remain functional even if a primary MFA service experiences downtime. Offline authentication mechanisms, including smart card-based authentication and emergency backup codes, provide contingency options for users in disaster recovery scenarios where internet-based MFA services are unavailable.

IAM business continuity planning requires automated failover mechanisms that minimize disruption to authentication and access control workflows. Organizations should leverage identity orchestration platforms that detect IAM service failures and automatically reroute authentication requests to alternative identity providers or backup authentication endpoints. Zero Trust architectures enhance IAM resilience by enforcing continuous authentication and adaptive access policies, ensuring that users and workloads remain authenticated even if a primary IAM service becomes temporarily unavailable.

Global IAM resilience strategies must account for regulatory and compliance considerations, ensuring that identity recovery mechanisms align with legal data protection requirements. Organizations operating across multiple jurisdictions must ensure that IAM backup and disaster recovery processes comply with data sovereignty laws, such as GDPR, CCPA, and China's Cybersecurity Law. Identity replication and failover configurations should respect regional access controls, preventing unauthorized cross-border data transfers while maintaining compliance with industry regulations.

Incident response planning for IAM disruptions must include predefined recovery playbooks, escalation procedures, and automated remediation workflows. Security teams must conduct regular IAM disaster recovery drills, simulating IAM failures, credential compromise scenarios, and federation outages to test response effectiveness. IAM recovery exercises should include role-based access restoration, identity validation procedures, and security incident logging to ensure rapid recovery with minimal security exposure.

IAM observability and monitoring play a critical role in early detection of identity service failures and malicious activity targeting IAM components. Organizations should integrate IAM logs with Security Information and Event Management (SIEM) platforms, allowing security teams to detect authentication anomalies, failed federation attempts, and unauthorized privilege escalations in real time. User and Entity Behavior Analytics (UEBA) enhances IAM security by identifying deviations from normal authentication patterns, enabling proactive threat mitigation before IAM disruptions escalate into major incidents.

IAM disaster recovery strategies must also address machine identities and service-to-service authentication. Many enterprise applications rely on machine identities, including API keys, service accounts, and cloud workload identities, to authenticate with backend services. Organizations must ensure that IAM failover mechanisms extend to machine identities, preventing disruptions in automated workflows, CI/CD pipelines, and microservices authentication. Implementing just-in-time machine identity issuance and workload identity federation ensures that service-to-service authentication remains secure and uninterrupted during IAM recovery processes.

IAM automation and Infrastructure-as-Code (IaC) play a critical role in business continuity planning, enabling organizations to rapidly redeploy IAM configurations in disaster recovery scenarios. Terraform, AWS CloudFormation, and Azure Bicep can be used to define IAM policies, roles, and identity federation settings as code, ensuring that IAM environments can be restored programmatically in the event of a failure. By integrating IAM disaster recovery plans with IaC workflows, organizations achieve rapid recovery with minimal manual intervention.

By designing IAM disaster recovery and business continuity strategies with high availability, failover automation, and regulatory compliance, global organizations can ensure that authentication, authorization, and identity governance remain resilient against disruptions. IAM resilience protects business operations, mitigates security risks, and ensures that users, applications, and workloads can securely authenticate in the face of unforeseen challenges. As IAM threats continue to evolve, organizations must continuously refine and test their IAM disaster recovery plans, ensuring that identity security remains an integral part of enterprise-wide business continuity planning.

Cloud IAM Hardening: Architecting for Least Privilege and Zero Standing Privileges

Cloud Identity and Access Management (IAM) is a critical component of securing cloud infrastructure, workloads, and applications. Unlike traditional on-premises IAM, cloud IAM operates in highly dynamic environments where access permissions, identities, and authentication mechanisms must be continuously monitored and adjusted to mitigate security risks. One of the fundamental principles of cloud IAM hardening is enforcing least privilege access (LPA) and implementing zero standing privileges (ZSP) to ensure that users, applications, and services have only the minimal permissions necessary for their tasks. By architecting cloud IAM with strict access controls, automated privilege escalation workflows, and continuous monitoring, organizations can significantly reduce the risk of unauthorized access, privilege escalation, and credential compromise.

Least privilege access (LPA) is a security principle that restricts identities to the bare minimum permissions required to perform specific tasks. Many security breaches occur due to excessive privileges granted to users, applications, and workloads, creating an attack surface that adversaries can exploit. In cloud environments, organizations must enforce LPA by implementing fine-grained IAM policies that define access permissions based on roles, attributes, and contextual factors. Instead of granting broad administrative privileges, cloud IAM policies should follow a granular access model where permissions are assigned based on job functions and operational needs.

Role-Based Access Control (RBAC) is commonly used to enforce least privilege access by assigning users to predefined roles with specific permissions. However, static role assignments often lead to privilege accumulation, where users retain permissions that are no longer necessary. To mitigate this risk, organizations should implement periodic access reviews and role recertification processes to ensure that identities maintain only the required permissions. Automated IAM governance tools can help enforce access reviews by detecting overprivileged identities and revoking unnecessary permissions.

Attribute-Based Access Control (ABAC) provides a more dynamic approach to least privilege enforcement by evaluating contextual attributes such as user department, device type, location, and security posture before granting access. Unlike RBAC, which relies on predefined role mappings, ABAC enables real-time access decisions based on dynamic conditions. Cloud IAM hardening should leverage ABAC to enforce conditional access policies, ensuring that access permissions are granted only when specific conditions are met. For example, a developer may be allowed to access a production environment only from a corporate-managed device and within predefined working hours.

Zero standing privileges (ZSP) is an advanced IAM strategy that eliminates persistent administrative access by granting privileged permissions only on a temporary basis. Traditional IAM models often assign long-term administrative privileges to users, increasing the risk of credential misuse and insider threats. In contrast, ZSP enforces just-in-time (JIT) access provisioning, where administrative privileges are granted only when needed and automatically revoked after a predefined period.

Implementing ZSP requires Privileged Access Management (PAM) solutions that support temporary privilege escalation and session monitoring. Cloud-native PAM services, such as AWS IAM Access Analyzer, Azure Privileged Identity Management (PIM), and Google Cloud IAM Recommender, enable organizations to implement just-in-time access policies for administrative roles. By integrating ZSP with PAM, organizations can ensure that privileged access is granted only for approved tasks and is continuously monitored to detect anomalies.

Service accounts and machine identities introduce unique challenges in cloud IAM hardening, as they often have excessive privileges that persist indefinitely. Many cloud workloads rely on service accounts to authenticate with APIs, databases, and third-party services, but these accounts are frequently overprivileged and lack proper lifecycle management. Organizations must implement strict governance policies for service accounts, ensuring that they adhere to least privilege principles and follow ZSP best practices.

To reduce the risk of service account compromise, organizations should enforce the use of short-lived credentials instead of static API keys or long-lived tokens. Cloud IAM hardening strategies should integrate workload identity federation mechanisms, such as AWS IAM Roles for Service Accounts (IRSA), Google Cloud Workload Identity Federation, and Azure Managed Identities, to enable secure authentication without exposing credentials. By eliminating hardcoded credentials and enforcing automatic credential rotation, organizations can minimize the attack surface associated with machine identities.

Multi-factor authentication (MFA) is a critical control for enforcing cloud IAM security and preventing unauthorized access to privileged accounts. While MFA is commonly enforced for human users, organizations must also implement MFA-equivalent controls for non-human identities, including service accounts and automated workloads. Adaptive authentication mechanisms should dynamically require step-up authentication when high-risk access attempts are detected, such as logins from untrusted networks or unusual geolocations.

IAM logging and monitoring play a crucial role in cloud IAM hardening by providing visibility into access patterns, privilege escalations, and anomalous authentication attempts. Cloud IAM services should be integrated with Security Information and Event Management (SIEM) platforms to enable real-time identity threat detection. IAM logs should capture key security events, including failed authentication attempts, privilege changes, and policy modifications. Implementing User and Entity Behavior Analytics (UEBA) enhances IAM security by detecting abnormal access behaviors that may indicate credential compromise or insider threats.

Cloud IAM policies should also incorporate identity lifecycle automation to enforce least privilege and ZSP at scale. Automated identity provisioning and deprovisioning workflows ensure that users and workloads receive appropriate permissions at onboarding and that access is revoked immediately upon termination. Cloud IAM automation tools, such as Terraform IAM modules, AWS Control Tower, and Azure Blueprints, enable organizations to enforce consistent identity policies across cloud environments while reducing manual IAM misconfigurations.

Securing cloud IAM also requires enforcing API security controls to prevent unauthorized access to IAM configurations and authentication tokens. Many cloud breaches occur due to exposed API credentials and improperly secured IAM management endpoints. Organizations should implement API security best practices, including OAuth2 authentication for API requests, rate limiting for IAM API calls, and API gateway enforcement to restrict access to IAM management functions.

Regular IAM policy audits and security baselines are essential for maintaining IAM hardening over time. Cloud IAM policies should be continuously reviewed and updated to align with emerging security threats, compliance requirements, and evolving business needs. Cloud IAM security posture management (CSPM) tools provide automated policy analysis, detecting misconfigured IAM permissions, excessive privileges, and unused access credentials. By leveraging CSPM solutions, organizations can proactively remediate IAM risks before they are exploited by attackers.

By architecting cloud IAM for least privilege and zero standing privileges, organizations can significantly reduce the risk of identity-based attacks, insider threats, and unauthorized access to cloud resources. Enforcing fine-grained access controls, implementing just-in-time privilege escalation, and continuously monitoring IAM activities ensure that cloud environments remain secure, resilient, and compliant with security best practices. As cloud IAM continues to evolve, organizations must adopt automation, policy-driven governance, and adaptive authentication to maintain strong identity security across multi-cloud and hybrid environments.

Architecting User-Centric IAM: Privacy by Design and Regulatory Compliance

Identity and Access Management (IAM) is no longer solely about securing authentication and authorization processes; it must also prioritize user privacy, data protection, and regulatory compliance. As enterprises collect and process vast amounts of personal and sensitive data, IAM architectures must incorporate Privacy by Design (PbD) principles to ensure that identity data is handled responsibly, securely, and transparently. Regulations such as the General Data Protection Regulation (GDPR), the California Consumer Privacy Act (CCPA), and other global privacy laws mandate strict IAM policies that enforce user consent, minimize data collection, and provide individuals with greater control over their digital identities. Designing a user-centric IAM framework requires embedding privacy controls at every stage of the identity lifecycle, from user onboarding to authentication, authorization, and identity governance.

Privacy by Design in IAM focuses on implementing identity solutions that minimize the collection and exposure of personal data while maintaining security and usability. Unlike traditional IAM models that prioritize enterprise security needs over user privacy, user-centric IAM ensures that individuals retain control over their personal information through consent-driven authentication, anonymization techniques, and data minimization policies. IAM solutions must be architected to process only the minimum required personal data needed for authentication and access control, reducing the risk of data breaches and regulatory non-compliance.

Consent management is a fundamental requirement of user-centric IAM, ensuring that users explicitly authorize how their identity data is used and shared. IAM systems must provide transparent consent mechanisms that allow users to opt in or opt out of data sharing, control third-party access, and manage authentication preferences. Implementing fine-grained consent controls enables users to grant or revoke access to specific identity attributes for different applications, ensuring compliance with privacy regulations. Identity providers (IdPs) should integrate consent management platforms (CMPs) that record and enforce user consent preferences, providing audit trails to demonstrate regulatory compliance.

Data minimization is another core principle of privacy-centric IAM, ensuring that only essential identity attributes are collected, processed, and stored. Traditional IAM systems often accumulate large amounts of personal data, increasing the risk of data exposure. Modern IAM architectures must implement Just-In-Time (JIT) identity provisioning, where identity attributes are requested only when required and discarded after the authentication session. Decentralized identity models, such as Self-Sovereign Identity (SSI) and verifiable credentials, enhance data minimization by allowing users to authenticate using cryptographic proofs rather than sharing raw personal data.

Regulatory compliance requires IAM solutions to enforce strict data retention and deletion policies. Many privacy laws mandate that organizations must not retain personal data longer than necessary for its intended purpose. IAM systems must support automated identity data lifecycle management, ensuring that personal data is anonymized, pseudonymized, or deleted based on regulatory retention requirements. Role-based access control (RBAC) and attribute-based access control (ABAC) should be applied to enforce access restrictions on sensitive identity attributes, ensuring that only authorized entities can view or modify personal data.

User access transparency is a key requirement for privacy compliance, enabling individuals to monitor how their identity data is used and who has accessed their accounts. IAM platforms must provide self-service identity portals where users can view access logs, manage authentication settings, and review consent history. Implementing privacy dashboards enhances user trust by offering real-time visibility into authentication attempts, consented data-sharing agreements, and security settings. Strong identity verification mechanisms, such as multi-factor authentication (MFA) and passwordless authentication, further protect user accounts while maintaining privacy compliance.

Identity federation and Single Sign-On (SSO) must be designed with privacy safeguards to prevent unnecessary data exposure during authentication. Many federated IAM models involve identity providers sharing user attributes with third-party applications, raising concerns about data propagation and unintended identity tracking. Privacy-preserving identity federation techniques, such as OpenID Connect (OIDC) selective attribute disclosure and OAuth2 token scoping, enable organizations to enforce least privilege access to identity attributes. Organizations must implement policy-based identity sharing agreements that limit the transmission of personal data to only what is strictly necessary for authentication.

Anonymization and pseudonymization techniques enhance IAM privacy by replacing personally identifiable information (PII) with cryptographic identifiers or tokenized values. Privacy-enhancing technologies (PETs), such as homomorphic encryption, zero-knowledge proofs (ZKPs), and differential privacy, enable IAM platforms to verify user identities without exposing sensitive data. For example, a financial institution could verify a user's age for age-restricted services without requiring access to the full date of birth by using verifiable credentials issued by trusted authorities. By adopting anonymization strategies, organizations reduce compliance risks while maintaining authentication accuracy.

Privacy-centric IAM architectures must also address security challenges related to data breaches, insider threats, and unauthorized identity correlation. IAM logging and monitoring solutions should be designed to detect unauthorized access attempts while minimizing the collection of sensitive identity metadata. Implementing pseudonymous logging ensures that authentication events can be audited without exposing personal identifiers, balancing security visibility with privacy protection. Integration with Security Information and Event Management (SIEM) platforms enables organizations to correlate identity events with broader security incidents while adhering to data protection regulations.

Zero Trust IAM principles align with Privacy by Design by enforcing continuous identity verification and contextual access control without relying on implicit trust assumptions. Instead of granting static, long-term access permissions, Zero Trust IAM dynamically evaluates user context, device trust, and authentication risk before allowing access. Implementing dynamic risk-based authentication (RBA) ensures that access decisions are made in real time based on behavioral analytics and threat intelligence. By continuously verifying identity attributes without persistent tracking, Zero Trust IAM enhances security while minimizing privacy risks.

IAM compliance automation is essential for reducing the administrative burden of meeting privacy regulations. Organizations must integrate compliance-as-code frameworks that automatically enforce regulatory IAM policies across cloud environments, SaaS applications, and on-premises identity systems. By leveraging policy engines such as Open Policy Agent (OPA) and regulatory compliance scanners, IAM teams can ensure that access control policies, consent management configurations, and data retention rules comply with legal mandates. Automated compliance reporting enables security teams to generate audit-ready IAM logs, demonstrating adherence to GDPR, CCPA, and industry-specific privacy standards.

Cross-border data transfer regulations introduce additional challenges for IAM privacy compliance, as many jurisdictions impose restrictions on how personal data can be stored and accessed across international borders. Organizations must implement geo-aware IAM policies that enforce data residency requirements, ensuring that authentication and identity storage comply with local laws. Multi-region IAM architectures should include encryption controls, regionalized identity providers, and consent-driven data-sharing agreements to mitigate cross-border data transfer risks.

By architecting user-centric IAM with Privacy by Design and regulatory compliance, organizations build trust with users while meeting global data protection requirements. Implementing privacy-first authentication, dynamic access controls, and consent-driven identity governance ensures that IAM systems protect user data while enabling secure and compliant access management. As regulatory landscapes evolve, enterprises must continuously enhance IAM privacy frameworks to adapt to emerging data protection laws, safeguard personal identity information, and uphold digital trust in an increasingly interconnected world.

Multi-Tenancy IAM Architectures for SaaS and Cloud Service Providers

Identity and Access Management (IAM) in multi-tenant architectures is a critical challenge for Software-as-a-Service (SaaS) and cloud service providers. Unlike traditional IAM models that manage identities within a single enterprise, multi-tenancy requires IAM to support multiple isolated tenants while ensuring security, scalability, and compliance. SaaS applications must enforce strong identity separation, fine-grained access controls, and dynamic authentication mechanisms to prevent unauthorized cross-tenant access and privilege escalation. Architecting a robust multi-tenancy IAM framework requires careful design considerations, including tenant identity isolation, federated authentication, role delegation, and centralized identity governance.

Multi-tenancy IAM architectures must ensure strict tenant isolation to prevent data leakage and unauthorized access between tenants. In a shared cloud environment, IAM must enforce logical separation between tenants, ensuring that users from one tenant cannot view, modify, or access resources belonging to another. Isolation can be achieved through identity namespaces, dedicated tenant directories, or policy-based access controls. Organizations should implement per-tenant identity segmentation by using unique identity realms, ensuring that authentication requests are validated against the correct tenant-specific identity store. Cloud-native IAM solutions, such as AWS Organizations, Azure AD B2C, and Google Cloud Identity, provide tenant-aware identity federation that ensures user authentication and authorization are scoped to the appropriate tenant.

Authentication in multi-tenant IAM architectures must support both native user authentication and federated identity models. SaaS providers often cater to customers with different identity management preferences, requiring support for enterprise Single Sign-On (SSO), social login, and multi-factor authentication (MFA). OpenID Connect (OIDC), SAML, and OAuth2 allow SaaS applications to integrate with external identity providers (IdPs), enabling seamless authentication without requiring users to create separate credentials. SaaS applications must implement dynamic authentication policies that adjust authentication mechanisms based on tenant-specific security requirements, allowing each customer to configure authentication preferences while maintaining IAM consistency across the platform.

Authorization models in multi-tenant IAM must provide flexible role delegation and fine-grained access controls. Role-Based Access Control (RBAC) is commonly used to define tenant-wide roles such as administrators, managers, and users. However, static role assignments may not provide sufficient flexibility for complex SaaS environments. Attribute-Based Access Control (ABAC) enhances multi-tenancy IAM by incorporating contextual attributes such as tenant ID, subscription level, and user department to dynamically grant or restrict access. Policy-Based Access Control (PBAC) further refines access management by enforcing centralized policies that evaluate user roles, resource ownership, and security posture before authorizing access.

Tenant-specific IAM configurations must be customizable without compromising security or scalability. SaaS providers must allow each tenant to define its own access policies, authentication requirements, and user provisioning workflows while ensuring that IAM enforcement remains standardized across all tenants. Implementing tenant-aware policy engines enables organizations to define global security policies while allowing per-tenant overrides. For example, one tenant may require step-up authentication for financial transactions, while another may enforce strict IP whitelisting for administrative access. IAM platforms must support policy inheritance, where global security rules apply across all tenants but can be customized at the tenant level to meet individual security requirements.

Multi-tenancy IAM must support delegated administration, allowing tenant-specific administrators to manage users, roles, and permissions within their own organizations. SaaS providers should implement hierarchical IAM structures where global platform administrators maintain control over IAM configurations while tenant administrators manage user provisioning and access control for their respective tenants. Delegated administration reduces operational overhead for the SaaS provider while empowering customers to self-manage IAM policies. Implementing tenant-scoped administrative roles ensures that delegated administrators cannot modify IAM settings beyond their assigned scope, preventing privilege escalation and unauthorized modifications.

User provisioning and identity lifecycle management in multi-tenancy IAM require automation and integration with tenant identity systems. SaaS applications must support System for Cross-domain Identity Management (SCIM) to enable automated user provisioning, role assignments, and deprovisioning. SCIM allows enterprises to synchronize user identities between their corporate directory and the SaaS provider's IAM system, ensuring that user accounts are automatically created, updated, or removed based on HR-driven identity changes. Just-in-Time (JIT) provisioning further enhances identity lifecycle automation by dynamically creating user accounts upon first login, reducing administrative effort and streamlining user onboarding. ———

Multi-tenant IAM architectures must enforce strong security measures to mitigate insider threats, identity fraud, and privilege misuse. SaaS providers should implement Zero Trust IAM principles, requiring continuous identity verification and adaptive access controls based on real-time risk assessments. User and Entity Behavior Analytics (UEBA) enhances IAM security by detecting anomalies such as excessive privilege escalations, suspicious access patterns, and failed authentication attempts across tenants. By integrating IAM with Security Information and Event Management (SIEM) platforms, organizations can monitor identity-related security events, enforce real-time threat response, and ensure compliance with security best practices.

Data residency and compliance considerations are critical for multi-tenant IAM in SaaS environments. Many enterprises operate in regulated industries that impose strict data sovereignty and privacy requirements, restricting how identity data is stored and accessed across geographic regions. SaaS providers must implement multi-region IAM architectures that enforce data localization policies, ensuring that user authentication data remains within designated jurisdictions. Compliance-driven IAM policies should support per-tenant regulatory configurations, allowing organizations to customize data retention policies, consent management workflows, and identity audit logging based on industry-specific mandates such as GDPR, HIPAA, and SOC 2.

API security is a key component of multi-tenancy IAM, ensuring that tenant-specific authentication and authorization mechanisms are securely exposed through IAM APIs. SaaS providers must implement OAuth2 client credentials flow, API gateways, and rate-limiting controls to prevent unauthorized API access and identity abuse. Tenant-aware API authentication ensures that API calls are scoped to the correct tenant, preventing cross-tenant data access and API abuse. Mutual TLS (mTLS) authentication further strengthens API security by ensuring that only authorized clients can communicate with IAM services.

Scalability is a fundamental requirement for multi-tenant IAM, as SaaS platforms must support millions of users and dynamic IAM policy evaluations across multiple tenants. IAM architectures should leverage distributed identity stores, caching mechanisms, and load-balanced authentication endpoints to ensure high availability and low-latency authentication requests. Edge-based authentication proxies and Content Delivery Network (CDN)-backed IAM services improve performance by reducing authentication round trips, ensuring seamless user experiences for globally distributed tenants.

Auditability and IAM governance in multi-tenant environments require comprehensive logging and reporting mechanisms. SaaS providers must provide tenants with visibility into authentication events, access logs, and privilege changes while maintaining strict tenant data separation. Implementing tenant-aware logging ensures that each organization can audit its own IAM activities without exposing sensitive identity data from other tenants. IAM governance dashboards allow administrators to track user access trends, enforce periodic access reviews, and detect policy violations in real time.

By architecting IAM for multi-tenancy in SaaS and cloud service providers, organizations achieve secure, scalable, and flexible identity management that meets the needs of diverse customer bases. Enforcing tenant isolation, supporting federated authentication, implementing fine-grained access control, and ensuring compliance-driven IAM policies enable SaaS providers to deliver secure and customizable IAM experiences. As multi-tenancy IAM evolves, SaaS platforms must continuously enhance identity security, automation, and interoperability to maintain trust and compliance in dynamic cloud environments.

IAM Decision Engines: Architecting Policy-Based Access Control (PBAC)

Identity and Access Management (IAM) is evolving beyond static role assignments and predefined permissions to support dynamic, real-time access control models. Policy-Based Access Control (PBAC) introduces a more flexible and context-aware authorization framework that evaluates policies at runtime to determine access decisions. Unlike traditional Role-Based Access Control (RBAC), which assigns permissions based on static roles, PBAC dynamically assesses contextual attributes, risk factors, and business policies to enforce fine-grained access control. Architecting IAM decision engines for PBAC requires implementing scalable policy evaluation frameworks, integrating contextual data sources, and ensuring policy consistency across distributed environments.

A PBAC-based IAM decision engine operates by processing structured policies that define access conditions based on attributes, rules, and real-time contextual signals. These policies are evaluated during authentication and authorization requests to determine whether a user, application, or machine identity should be granted access to a resource. PBAC provides a higher degree of flexibility than RBAC, allowing security teams to enforce conditional access policies that adapt to changing user behavior, risk profiles, and regulatory requirements.

The core components of a PBAC IAM decision engine include Policy Decision Points (PDPs), Policy Enforcement Points (PEPs), and Policy Information Points (PIPs). PDPs are responsible for evaluating access control policies against incoming access requests, determining whether access should be granted or denied. PEPs enforce policy decisions by intercepting authentication and authorization requests at the application, API gateway, or network layer. PIPs provide external contextual data sources, such as identity attributes, risk scores, and environmental conditions, that are used to enrich policy evaluations. Together, these components create a real-time decision-making framework that enhances access security while reducing administrative overhead.

PBAC policies are typically defined using declarative policy languages such as eXtensible Access Control Markup Language (XACML) or Open Policy Agent (OPA) Rego. These policies describe access rules in terms of attributes, conditions, and obligations that must be met before access is granted. For example, a PBAC policy for financial transactions may enforce a rule stating that only users with the role of "Manager" can approve transactions exceeding $10,000, but only if they are accessing the system from a corporate network and have passed multi-factor authentication within the last 15 minutes. By defining access rules using structured policies, organizations achieve consistent, auditable, and reusable authorization logic across multiple systems.

Context-aware access control is a key advantage of PBAC, enabling security teams to enforce dynamic access decisions based on risk signals and environmental factors. Unlike RBAC, which relies on static role assignments, PBAC allows organizations to incorporate factors such as geolocation, device security posture, login behavior, and session attributes into access evaluations. For example, a PBAC policy might require step-up authentication if a user attempts to access sensitive data from an unmanaged device or a high-risk location. This approach strengthens security by adapting access controls to real-time conditions rather than relying on predefined role mappings.

PBAC enhances Zero Trust IAM architectures by enforcing continuous authentication and dynamic access control policies. In traditional IAM models, access permissions are granted at login and remain valid for the duration of a session. However, PBAC enables continuous policy evaluation, allowing IAM systems to revoke access dynamically if security conditions change. For instance, if an authenticated user suddenly switches to an untrusted network or exhibits suspicious behavior, a PBAC decision engine can automatically trigger session termination or require additional authentication. This continuous evaluation process ensures that access decisions remain aligned with security policies at all times.

Multi-cloud and hybrid IAM environments benefit significantly from PBAC, as organizations can enforce consistent access policies across diverse cloud platforms, SaaS applications, and on-premises systems. Traditional IAM models often require platform-specific role mappings and permission assignments, leading to inconsistencies and security gaps. PBAC eliminates these challenges by centralizing policy enforcement, ensuring that access decisions are evaluated uniformly across different environments. Cloud-native policy engines, such as AWS IAM Policy Simulator, Azure Role-Based Access Control (RBAC) with conditions, and Google Cloud IAM Conditions, support policy-driven authorization frameworks that align with PBAC principles.

IAM decision engines for PBAC must integrate with identity analytics and risk-based access control (RBAC) to enhance adaptive security. By leveraging risk intelligence from SIEM platforms, User and Entity Behavior Analytics (UEBA), and threat detection systems, PBAC policies can incorporate dynamic risk assessments into access decisions. For example, an IAM decision engine may block access to a critical system if a user's risk score exceeds a predefined threshold based on behavioral anomalies, recent failed login attempts, or known threat indicators. This integration ensures that access control policies remain responsive to evolving security threats.

Auditability and compliance are key drivers for PBAC adoption, as organizations must demonstrate that access decisions align with regulatory requirements. PBAC policies provide a transparent and auditable mechanism for enforcing data access controls, enabling security teams to generate detailed access logs, policy evaluation reports, and compliance attestations. Organizations subject to GDPR, HIPAA, PCI-DSS, and SOX regulations can use PBAC to enforce granular data protection policies, ensuring that only authorized users can access sensitive information under predefined conditions.

Performance and scalability considerations are critical when designing PBAC IAM decision engines, as policy evaluations must occur in real time without introducing authentication latency. To optimize performance, organizations should implement distributed policy evaluation architectures that leverage caching, edge-based policy enforcement, and parallelized decision processing. Policy evaluation engines should be designed to handle high-throughput authorization requests while maintaining low-latency response times to support large-scale enterprise IAM deployments.

Integration with modern application architectures, including microservices and API-driven ecosystems, further enhances the effectiveness of PBAC. IAM decision engines must provide API-based policy evaluation endpoints that allow applications, CI/CD pipelines, and containerized workloads to query authorization policies dynamically. Implementing PBAC at the API gateway level ensures that service-to-service authentication and machine identity authorization are governed by the same policy framework as human user authentication.

Organizations adopting PBAC must also focus on policy lifecycle management, ensuring that access policies remain up to date, optimized, and aligned with business requirements. IAM teams should implement automated policy validation pipelines that continuously test and refine access control policies to prevent misconfigurations, overprivileged access, and policy conflicts. Machine learning and AI-driven policy optimization techniques can further enhance PBAC by recommending policy adjustments based on observed access patterns and risk assessments.

By architecting IAM decision engines for PBAC, organizations achieve a dynamic, scalable, and context-aware access control framework that enhances security, improves regulatory compliance, and supports adaptive access management. PBAC enables enterprises to move beyond static role assignments, implementing intelligent access control policies that evolve in real time based on risk, user context, and security conditions. As organizations continue adopting cloud-native architectures, Zero Trust security models, and API-driven ecosystems, PBAC will play an increasingly critical role in ensuring that IAM remains flexible, secure, and aligned with modern business requirements.

IAM in Edge Computing: Architecting Identity for IoT and 5G Networks

Identity and Access Management (IAM) in edge computing environments presents unique challenges compared to traditional IAM architectures. The rapid expansion of Internet of Things (IoT) devices, 5G networks, and distributed cloud computing has created a decentralized security landscape where identities must be managed beyond the enterprise perimeter. Unlike centralized IAM models, which rely on cloud-based or on-premises identity providers, edge computing demands identity solutions that operate across geographically dispersed locations with intermittent connectivity and varying levels of security. Architecting IAM for edge environments requires a scalable, resilient, and low-latency approach to authenticating users, devices, and services while enforcing fine-grained access controls in highly dynamic and resource-constrained settings.

Edge computing moves processing power closer to data sources, reducing latency and bandwidth consumption. However, this decentralization also introduces identity-related risks, such as unauthorized device access, insecure authentication mechanisms, and a larger attack surface for identity threats. IoT devices operating at the edge often have limited computational capabilities, making it challenging to implement traditional IAM security measures, such as public-key infrastructure (PKI), complex cryptographic operations, or centralized identity federation. To secure edge environments, IAM architectures must incorporate lightweight authentication protocols, decentralized identity management, and self-sovereign identity (SSI) models that enable edge nodes to operate independently of centralized IAM systems.

IoT identity management is a critical aspect of IAM in edge computing. Unlike human identities, which are managed through usernames, passwords, and multi-factor authentication (MFA), IoT devices authenticate using machine identities, digital certificates, and secure hardware modules. Each IoT device must be uniquely identifiable to prevent unauthorized devices from gaining access to edge networks. Organizations should implement device attestation techniques, such as Trusted Platform Modules (TPMs) and Hardware Security Modules

(HSMs), to verify the authenticity of edge devices before granting network access. Mutual authentication using device certificates and challenge-response mechanisms ensures that only authorized devices can interact with edge infrastructure.

5G networks introduce additional complexity to IAM by enabling ultra-low-latency communication, network slicing, and massive device connectivity. Traditional IAM models are not designed to handle the scale and speed of 5G networks, requiring identity solutions that can authenticate and authorize millions of devices in real time. Cloud-native IAM services, such as AWS IoT Core, Azure IoT Hub, and Google Cloud IoT, provide identity federation and secure access management for edge devices, but organizations must also consider decentralized IAM models to support autonomous edge deployments. Federated identity frameworks, such as Decentralized Identifiers (DIDs) and Verifiable Credentials (VCs), allow edge devices to authenticate without relying on centralized identity providers, reducing dependency on cloud-based IAM systems.

IAM in edge computing must support Zero Trust security principles, where every device, user, and application is continuously authenticated and authorized based on dynamic security policies. Unlike traditional network perimeter security, which assumes implicit trust for internal devices, Zero Trust IAM enforces least privilege access by verifying identity attributes, geolocation, and device trustworthiness before granting permissions. Implementing Zero Trust in edge environments requires identity-aware network policies that control access based on real-time risk assessments. Policy-Based Access Control (PBAC) and Attribute-Based Access Control (ABAC) provide fine-grained authorization at the edge, ensuring that only trusted entities can interact with critical resources.

IAM resilience is a crucial requirement for edge deployments, as intermittent connectivity and network outages can disrupt authentication services. Traditional IAM systems rely on cloud-based identity providers, but edge environments require identity mechanisms that function in offline or low-bandwidth scenarios. Edge IAM solutions should incorporate caching strategies, such as pre-issued authentication tokens, locally stored identity credentials, and decentralized blockchain-based identity ledgers. These approaches allow edge devices to verify identity even when disconnected from central IAM systems, ensuring continuous access to mission-critical applications.

Micro-segmentation and identity-based network access control enhance IAM security in 5G and edge environments. Instead of relying on static firewall rules or VPN-based access, organizations should implement software-defined perimeter (SDP) architectures that dynamically enforce identity-aware network segmentation. Edge nodes, IoT gateways, and 5G base stations must authenticate using mutual TLS (mTLS) and zero-trust network access (ZTNA) protocols, ensuring that devices can only communicate with authorized services. By integrating IAM with network security policies, organizations reduce the risk of lateral movement attacks and unauthorized data access.

Machine learning and artificial intelligence (AI) play an essential role in IAM threat detection at the edge. Centralized SIEM (Security Information and Event Management) platforms often struggle to monitor distributed edge environments, requiring AI-driven anomaly detection models that operate locally. Edge AI-based identity analytics detect unauthorized authentication attempts, privilege escalation attempts, and device behavior anomalies in real time. Implementing User and Entity Behavior Analytics (UEBA) at the edge enhances security by continuously learning and adapting to evolving identity threats without relying on constant cloud connectivity.

IAM logging and auditing must be adapted for edge computing environments to ensure regulatory compliance and forensic analysis. Unlike centralized IAM logs, which are stored in cloud SIEMs, edge identity logs must be collected, encrypted, and synchronized with central IAM systems when network connectivity is available. Organizations should implement lightweight log aggregation protocols, such as Fluentd and OpenTelemetry, to ensure that authentication events, access control decisions, and privilege escalations are securely transmitted from edge devices to centralized logging systems. End-to-end encryption and tamper-proof storage ensure that IAM logs remain protected from insider threats and data manipulation.

Interoperability is another key consideration for IAM in edge and 5G environments. Organizations deploying edge infrastructure across multiple vendors, cloud platforms, and telecom providers must ensure that IAM solutions support open authentication and authorization standards. OpenID Connect (OIDC) and OAuth2 provide federated authentication capabilities for edge devices, while SCIM (System for Cross-domain Identity Management) ensures seamless user and device provisioning across edge IAM platforms. Implementing identity interoperability frameworks allows organizations to integrate third-party IoT devices, industrial control systems (ICS), and 5G network slices without compromising security.

Regulatory compliance remains a challenge for IAM in edge computing, as many industries impose strict identity security requirements for IoT devices and distributed computing. Organizations in healthcare, finance, and critical infrastructure sectors must ensure that edge IAM aligns with regulatory mandates such as GDPR, HIPAA, and NIST 800-207 (Zero Trust Architecture). IAM solutions must enforce strict data sovereignty policies, ensuring that identity data collected at the edge complies with regional data protection laws. Implementing encryption-at-rest and encryption-in-transit for identity credentials ensures that sensitive identity information remains protected, even in highly distributed environments.

By architecting IAM for edge computing, organizations enable secure, scalable, and resilient identity management across IoT, 5G networks, and distributed cloud environments. Implementing decentralized identity models, Zero Trust security principles, and adaptive authentication mechanisms ensures that edge IAM remains robust against emerging cyber threats. As the adoption of edge computing accelerates, IAM strategies must continue evolving to support the next generation of identity security challenges in highly dynamic and interconnected environments.

Global IAM Deployment Strategies: Centralized vs. Distributed Architectures

Identity and Access Management (IAM) is a foundational component of enterprise security, enabling organizations to control authentication, authorization, and identity governance across users, applications, and infrastructure. As enterprises expand globally, IAM must be designed to scale across multiple geographic regions, regulatory environments, and cloud platforms while maintaining security, performance, and compliance. Two primary IAM deployment strategies emerge in global organizations: centralized IAM and distributed IAM architectures. Choosing between these approaches requires a careful evaluation of factors such as operational efficiency, regulatory compliance, latency, resilience, and administrative complexity.

A centralized IAM architecture consolidates identity management functions into a single, globally managed IAM system. In this model, authentication services, identity providers (IdPs), access control policies, and user directories are centrally managed in one or more core data centers or cloud IAM platforms. This approach simplifies identity administration by providing a unified identity source, enforcing consistent security policies, and reducing IAM infrastructure overhead. Centralized IAM is often deployed using cloud-native IAM services such as Azure Active Directory, AWS IAM, or Google Cloud Identity, enabling organizations to maintain a single identity authority across all business units and geographic locations.

Centralized IAM offers several advantages, including uniform security policy enforcement, simplified identity governance, and streamlined regulatory compliance. By managing identities in a single repository, organizations can apply consistent authentication mechanisms, such as Single Sign-On (SSO) and Multi-Factor Authentication (MFA), across all applications and services. Centralized IAM enhances visibility into access patterns and authentication logs, enabling security teams to monitor and audit user activities across the entire organization from a central location. Additionally, centralized IAM simplifies regulatory compliance by maintaining standardized identity policies, reducing the risk of inconsistent access controls that may lead to non-compliance with global data protection laws such as GDPR, CCPA, and HIPAA.

However, centralized IAM also presents challenges, particularly for global enterprises with distributed users and hybrid IT environments. A single, centrally managed IAM system may introduce latency issues for users in distant geographic regions, as authentication requests must traverse long network paths to reach the identity provider. This latency can negatively impact user experience, particularly in high-performance environments such as financial trading platforms or real-time collaboration applications. Additionally, centralized IAM architectures may become a single point of failure, where an outage in the core IAM system could disrupt authentication and access control for all users worldwide.

To mitigate these risks, organizations deploying centralized IAM must implement geo-redundant IAM architectures, ensuring that identity services are replicated across multiple regions with automatic failover mechanisms. Cloud IAM services typically offer multi-region deployments, allowing organizations to distribute authentication traffic while maintaining a single identity authority. By implementing IAM load balancing, edge authentication proxies, and global content delivery networks (CDNs), enterprises can optimize authentication performance while maintaining the benefits of centralized identity management.

In contrast, a distributed IAM architecture decentralizes identity management by deploying IAM services across multiple regional or local instances. In this model, each geographic region, business unit, or cloud environment may operate its own identity provider, authentication services, and access control policies while maintaining interoperability with the broader IAM ecosystem. Distributed IAM architectures are commonly adopted in multinational enterprises, government agencies, and organizations that operate in highly regulated industries with strict data residency requirements.

The primary advantage of distributed IAM is improved latency and performance, as authentication and authorization requests are processed locally rather than relying on a central identity provider. By deploying IAM services closer to users and applications, organizations can reduce authentication delays and improve response times for mission-critical workloads. Distributed IAM also enhances resilience and availability, as localized identity providers ensure that authentication services remain operational even if a regional outage affects the broader IAM infrastructure.

Another key benefit of distributed IAM is regulatory compliance and data sovereignty. Many governments impose restrictions on how identity data is stored, processed, and transferred across borders. Regulations such as the EU's GDPR, China's Cybersecurity Law, and Brazil's LGPD require organizations to ensure that user authentication data remains within specific geographic boundaries. A distributed IAM model allows enterprises to deploy region-specific identity providers that comply with local data protection laws while maintaining secure interoperability with the global IAM framework.

However, distributed IAM also introduces administrative complexity and potential security inconsistencies. Managing multiple identity providers across different regions requires careful coordination to ensure consistent security policies, identity synchronization, and user provisioning workflows. Organizations must implement robust federated IAM mechanisms, such as SAML-based trust relationships, OAuth2 token exchanges, and identity brokering, to enable seamless authentication and authorization across distributed identity domains. Without proper IAM governance, a distributed architecture can lead to identity fragmentation, where users have multiple identities across different regions, increasing the risk of misconfigured access controls and unauthorized privileges.

To address these challenges, organizations adopting distributed IAM should implement policy-driven identity federation, ensuring that each regional IAM instance adheres to global security standards while allowing for local policy customizations. Centralized IAM governance platforms, such as Identity Governance and Administration (IGA) tools, can provide visibility into access controls across distributed IAM instances, enabling organizations to enforce consistent role-based and attribute-based access policies at a global scale.

Hybrid IAM architectures combine elements of both centralized and distributed IAM models to balance security, performance, and compliance requirements. In a hybrid IAM approach, organizations maintain a globally managed identity provider for core authentication and identity governance while deploying regional IAM instances for localized authentication, regulatory compliance, and performance optimization. Hybrid IAM architectures leverage workload identity federation, where applications and services authenticate with regional identity providers while synchronizing identity metadata with the central IAM authority.

IAM automation plays a critical role in managing both centralized and distributed IAM architectures. Organizations should leverage Infrastructure-as-Code (IaC) tools such as Terraform, AWS CloudFormation, and Azure Bicep to automate the provisioning, configuration, and policy enforcement of IAM services across multiple environments. IAM automation ensures that identity policies remain synchronized across distributed IAM instances while reducing the operational overhead of manual IAM administration.

Security monitoring and IAM observability must be integrated into both centralized and distributed IAM models to detect identity threats, policy violations, and authentication anomalies. Organizations should implement User and Entity Behavior Analytics (UEBA) to monitor authentication patterns across global IAM deployments, identifying suspicious activity such as failed login attempts, unauthorized privilege escalations, and cross-region access anomalies. By correlating IAM logs with Security Information and Event Management (SIEM) platforms, organizations can enhance identity threat detection and incident response across their global IAM footprint.

By evaluating the strengths and challenges of centralized and distributed IAM architectures, organizations can design IAM strategies that align with their business goals, security requirements, and regulatory obligations. While centralized IAM provides uniform policy enforcement and administrative simplicity, distributed IAM enhances performance, resilience, and regulatory compliance. Enterprises must carefully assess their global IAM needs, leveraging automation, identity federation, and security monitoring to build a scalable, secure, and adaptive identity management framework that supports users, applications, and workloads across multiple regions.

IAM Analytics and Intelligence: Architecting Real-Time Identity Threat Detection

Identity and Access Management (IAM) analytics and intelligence have become essential components of enterprise security, enabling organizations to detect and respond to identity-based threats in real time. Traditional IAM systems focus on authentication and authorization, but without advanced analytics, they lack the capability to identify anomalies, detect compromised credentials, and prevent unauthorized access. IAM analytics leverages machine learning, behavioral analysis, and real-time threat intelligence to monitor authentication activities, privilege escalations, and access patterns across users, devices, and applications. By architecting IAM intelligence solutions, organizations can proactively mitigate identity threats, enforce dynamic access controls, and strengthen Zero Trust security models.

Real-time identity threat detection requires continuous monitoring of authentication logs, access control decisions, and privilege assignments. Unlike static IAM models, which rely on predefined role-based policies, modern IAM analytics evaluates identity behavior dynamically, detecting deviations from normal usage patterns. Organizations must implement Security Information and Event Management (SIEM) platforms, User and Entity Behavior Analytics (UEBA), and IAM-specific risk engines to analyze identity data streams in real time. These solutions integrate with IAM logs, Single Sign-On (SSO) events, and federated identity providers to create a comprehensive view of user authentication trends and access anomalies.

Behavioral analytics plays a key role in IAM intelligence, identifying abnormal authentication patterns that indicate potential security threats. Traditional authentication mechanisms only verify user credentials at login, but behavioral IAM continuously monitors user activity to detect suspicious behavior. If an employee typically accesses enterprise applications from New York during business hours but suddenly logs in from an untrusted location in a different country, IAM analytics can flag the session as high-risk and trigger an adaptive response. Machine learning models analyze historical authentication data, creating behavioral baselines for each identity and generating real-time risk scores when anomalies are detected.

Compromised credentials remain one of the most significant attack vectors in identity security breaches. IAM intelligence solutions integrate with threat intelligence feeds to detect credential leaks from dark web sources, data breaches, and phishing campaigns. When a user's credentials are found in a breach repository, IAM systems can automatically trigger forced password resets, revoke active authentication tokens, or enforce step-up authentication through Multi-Factor Authentication (MFA). By continuously scanning for exposed identity data, IAM analytics prevents attackers from exploiting stolen credentials to gain unauthorized access.

Privilege escalation detection is another critical function of IAM analytics, as attackers often attempt to escalate their access privileges to move laterally within an organization's infrastructure. IAM intelligence solutions monitor administrative role assignments, permission changes, and access control modifications to identify suspicious privilege escalations. If a standard user account suddenly gains administrative privileges without a valid justification, IAM analytics can trigger security alerts, revoke the privilege change, or require explicit approval from security administrators. Automated privilege monitoring ensures that unauthorized privilege escalations are detected and mitigated before they lead to data breaches or insider threats.

Real-time anomaly detection in IAM analytics also applies to API security, where machine identities and service-to-service authentication require continuous monitoring. Many cyberattacks exploit compromised API keys or improperly configured OAuth2 tokens to access sensitive enterprise data. IAM intelligence platforms monitor API authentication requests, detecting excessive token reuse, suspicious API call patterns, and anomalous service interactions. Implementing AI-driven anomaly detection for API authentication helps organizations identify and block unauthorized API access attempts before they lead to data exfiltration.

IAM threat detection extends beyond authentication events to continuous access monitoring, ensuring that security policies remain enforced throughout a user session. Adaptive authentication and risk-based access control (RBAC) dynamically adjust access permissions based on real-time risk assessments. If a previously authenticated user exhibits unusual behavior, such as accessing highly sensitive financial records outside of normal working hours, IAM analytics can enforce re-authentication, restrict access, or terminate the session entirely. By continuously evaluating authentication risk, organizations prevent identity threats from escalating into full-scale security incidents.

IAM analytics must also support Zero Trust security models, where no user or device is implicitly trusted, and every access request is continuously validated. Traditional IAM architectures grant access based on static roles, but Zero Trust IAM requires real-time verification of user identities, device integrity, and contextual risk factors before granting or maintaining access. IAM intelligence solutions enforce Zero Trust by analyzing real-time identity attributes, monitoring device telemetry, and correlating security events across multiple identity providers. Identity risk scoring ensures that access decisions are made dynamically, minimizing the risk of credential compromise and unauthorized access.

Security automation is essential for real-time IAM intelligence, enabling organizations to respond to identity threats without manual intervention. Security Orchestration, Automation, and Response (SOAR) platforms integrate with IAM analytics to automate threat remediation workflows. When IAM analytics detects suspicious authentication activity, SOAR systems can initiate automated responses such as disabling the compromised user account, revoking OAuth2 tokens, or initiating a forensic investigation. Automating IAM security responses accelerates incident containment, reducing the time attackers have to exploit identity vulnerabilities.

IAM observability enhances identity threat detection by aggregating authentication logs, access requests, and privilege changes into a unified analytics platform. Traditional IAM logging mechanisms generate large volumes of security data, but without proper observability, security teams struggle to extract actionable insights. IAM intelligence solutions integrate with OpenTelemetry, Fluentd, and SIEM platforms to provide centralized visibility into identity activities. Dashboards and real-time alerts allow security teams to quickly identify and respond to identity threats, reducing the attack surface and minimizing the impact of security incidents.

Organizations deploying IAM intelligence solutions must also consider compliance and regulatory requirements, ensuring that real-time threat detection aligns with industry security standards. Many regulations, such as GDPR, HIPAA, and PCI-DSS, require organizations to monitor identity activities, enforce access controls, and maintain audit logs of authentication events. IAM analytics platforms provide compliance dashboards, risk assessments, and automated reporting capabilities that enable organizations to demonstrate regulatory adherence. Implementing IAM threat detection with compliance automation ensures that identity security policies remain enforceable while meeting legal obligations.

The future of IAM analytics and intelligence lies in AI-driven identity security, where advanced machine learning models continuously adapt to emerging identity threats. Organizations must invest in AI-powered IAM solutions that analyze vast amounts of authentication data, detect unknown attack patterns, and predict future identity threats. By leveraging deep learning, predictive analytics, and federated identity intelligence, enterprises can proactively defend against evolving cyber threats while maintaining seamless user access. IAM intelligence must evolve alongside emerging identity security challenges, ensuring that organizations remain resilient against credential theft, privilege abuse, and sophisticated identity attacks in an increasingly digital landscape.

Identity-Defined Security: Architecting IAM for Converged Cybersecurity Frameworks

Identity and Access Management (IAM) is no longer just a support function for authentication and authorization; it has become a foundational pillar of modern cybersecurity frameworks. Traditional security models relied on perimeter-based defenses, but as organizations adopt cloud computing, Zero Trust principles, and hybrid IT environments, identity has become the new security perimeter. Identity-Defined Security (IDS) integrates IAM with broader cybersecurity strategies, ensuring that identity is a central component of threat detection, risk mitigation, and policy enforcement. Architecting IAM for converged cybersecurity frameworks requires a seamless fusion of authentication, authorization, threat intelligence, and security automation to create an adaptive, resilient, and policy-driven security model.

Identity-Defined Security shifts the focus from static access control models to dynamic, context-aware security enforcement. Unlike traditional IAM systems that grant access based on predefined roles and permissions, IDS continuously evaluates risk factors, user behavior, and real-time security signals to make adaptive access decisions. By integrating IAM with Security Information and Event Management (SIEM) platforms, Extended Detection and Response (XDR) solutions, and User and Entity Behavior Analytics (UEBA), organizations can enforce identity-driven security policies that respond to emerging threats in real time.

Zero Trust security architectures are a core principle of Identity-Defined Security, ensuring that no user, device, or workload is implicitly trusted. Zero Trust IAM continuously verifies identities, enforces least privilege access, and applies risk-based authentication based on contextual data. Instead of relying solely on static role assignments, IDS dynamically adjusts access controls based on factors such as geolocation, device trustworthiness, and behavioral analytics. If an identity exhibits anomalous behavior, IDS can trigger step-up authentication, revoke access, or apply stricter security controls in real time.

IAM in converged cybersecurity frameworks must integrate with endpoint security solutions, cloud security posture management (CSPM), and data loss prevention (DLP) tools to enforce consistent identity-based security policies. Endpoint security platforms, such as Microsoft Defender for Endpoint, CrowdStrike Falcon, and SentinelOne, provide telemetry on device health and security posture.

By integrating IAM with endpoint security data, organizations can enforce conditional access policies that restrict authentication if a device is compromised, running outdated software, or exhibiting suspicious activity. This convergence ensures that IAM policies adapt to real-time security conditions, preventing compromised identities from accessing critical resources.

Privileged Access Management (PAM) is a key component of Identity-Defined Security, ensuring that administrative accounts and high-risk privileges are protected from insider threats and credential compromise. Unlike traditional PAM solutions that rely on static access controls, IDS implements Just-In-Time (JIT) privilege escalation, where administrative access is granted only for specific tasks and revoked immediately after use. By integrating PAM with SIEM and IAM analytics, organizations can detect anomalous privileged access behavior and enforce automated security responses. Adaptive privilege management reduces the risk of lateral movement attacks, where attackers escalate privileges to compromise sensitive systems.

Multi-cloud security frameworks require identity federation and workload authentication to protect distributed applications and hybrid infrastructures. Identity-Defined Security ensures that IAM extends beyond human users to secure machine identities, API authentication, and cloud-to-cloud access. By integrating IAM with cloud security solutions such as AWS Identity Center, Azure AD Conditional Access, and Google Cloud BeyondCorp, organizations can enforce unified identity policies across diverse cloud environments. Identity-based security controls prevent unauthorized access to cloud workloads, ensuring that only trusted applications and services can interact with sensitive cloud resources.

Threat intelligence integration enhances IAM security by providing real-time risk assessments based on global cybersecurity threat feeds. Identity-Defined Security incorporates threat intelligence from sources such as MITRE ATT&CK, threat-sharing communities, and commercial threat intelligence providers to dynamically adjust access policies. If an IAM system detects that a user's credentials have been compromised in a known data breach, it can immediately force password rotation, invalidate authentication tokens, and enforce MFA revalidation. This proactive approach prevents attackers from exploiting stolen credentials before they can be used for unauthorized access.

Security automation and orchestration play a crucial role in Identity-Defined Security, enabling organizations to respond to identity threats with minimal manual intervention. Security Orchestration, Automation, and Response (SOAR) platforms integrate with IAM to automate incident response workflows. When an identity-based security event is detected, SOAR systems can automatically trigger remediation actions, such as isolating a compromised user account, revoking access tokens, or notifying security teams. Automating IAM security responses enhances the speed and efficiency of threat mitigation, reducing the window of opportunity for attackers.

Identity governance and compliance frameworks must align with Identity-Defined Security to ensure regulatory adherence and auditability. Many industries require strict access control policies, periodic access reviews, and identity lifecycle management to comply with regulations such as GDPR, HIPAA, PCI-DSS, and ISO 27001. IDS integrates IAM with Identity Governance and Administration (IGA) solutions, enabling organizations to enforce policy-driven access controls while maintaining compliance with security mandates. Automated identity governance ensures that access permissions are granted, reviewed, and revoked based on business policies and compliance requirements.

IAM observability and real-time analytics provide security teams with deep visibility into identity-related threats and authentication anomalies. Organizations must implement centralized IAM logging, identity threat dashboards, and continuous monitoring to detect unauthorized access attempts, privilege escalations, and insider threats. Identity-Defined Security incorporates machine learning-driven analytics to correlate IAM events with broader security incidents, enabling proactive security enforcement. Security teams can use identity observability to track authentication trends, detect emerging attack patterns, and refine IAM policies based on real-time security insights.

Securing API authentication and machine-to-machine identities is a critical aspect of IDS, as modern applications rely on microservices, serverless architectures, and API-driven integrations. API gateways and identity-aware proxies must enforce OAuth2 token validation, API access policies, and mutual TLS (mTLS) authentication to ensure that only authorized services can communicate with backend systems. Identity-Defined Security ensures that machine identities are continuously verified, preventing unauthorized API interactions and service impersonation attacks.

Future-proofing IAM for Identity-Defined Security requires organizations to adopt decentralized identity models, self-sovereign identity (SSI), and blockchain-based authentication. Decentralized identity solutions reduce reliance on centralized identity providers, giving users control over their digital identities while enabling verifiable credentials for authentication. Blockchain-based identity verification can enhance security by ensuring tamper-proof identity records, preventing identity fraud, and enabling cross-border identity federation.

By architecting IAM for Identity-Defined Security within converged cybersecurity frameworks, organizations create a unified approach to identity protection, threat detection, and policy enforcement. Integrating IAM with Zero Trust, endpoint security, cloud security, and threat intelligence enables real-time identity risk assessment and adaptive security responses. As cyber threats continue to evolve, Identity-Defined Security ensures that IAM remains at the forefront of modern security architectures, protecting users, applications, and workloads from identity-based attacks.

IAM as a Service (IDaaS): Architecting Managed IAM Solutions for Enterprises

Identity and Access Management (IAM) is a fundamental security pillar for enterprises, enabling secure authentication, authorization, and identity governance. However, managing on-premises IAM infrastructure can be complex, resource-intensive, and difficult to scale. Identity as a Service (IDaaS) offers a cloud-based approach to IAM, providing enterprises with managed authentication, access control, and identity federation capabilities without the burden of maintaining on-premises identity systems. IDaaS platforms streamline identity management by offering centralized identity storage, Single Sign-On (SSO), multi-factor authentication (MFA), and role-based access controls (RBAC) as fully managed services. Architecting IDaaS solutions for enterprises requires careful planning to ensure scalability, security, compliance, and seamless integration with existing IT ecosystems.

IDaaS solutions provide enterprises with a unified identity management framework that integrates with cloud applications, SaaS platforms, and on-premises resources. Unlike traditional IAM systems, which require dedicated infrastructure, IDaaS solutions operate as multi-tenant cloud services, offering elastic scalability and automated updates. Leading IDaaS providers, such as Microsoft Entra ID (formerly Azure AD), Okta, Ping Identity, and Google Cloud Identity, provide organizations with identity management capabilities that align with modern security best practices, including Zero Trust architectures and adaptive authentication.

A key advantage of IDaaS is its ability to provide federated identity management across multiple cloud environments and SaaS applications. Enterprises often manage identities across diverse ecosystems, requiring integration with third-party identity providers (IdPs) and directory services. IDaaS platforms support identity federation through Security Assertion Markup Language (SAML), OpenID Connect (OIDC), and OAuth2, enabling seamless authentication across multiple services without requiring separate credentials for each application. Federated SSO simplifies user authentication while reducing password sprawl, improving both security and user experience.

Multi-Factor Authentication (MFA) is a critical component of IDaaS, ensuring that user identities are verified through multiple authentication factors before granting access. IDaaS providers offer built-in MFA capabilities, including push notifications, SMS-based OTPs, biometric authentication, and hardware security keys such as FIDO2/WebAuthn. Adaptive MFA enhances security by applying risk-based authentication policies that dynamically require additional authentication factors when suspicious login attempts are detected.

Organizations can enforce step-up authentication for high-risk access requests, ensuring that privileged actions require stronger identity verification mechanisms.

IDaaS also supports Role-Based Access Control (RBAC) and Attribute-Based Access Control (ABAC), allowing enterprises to enforce granular access policies across applications and services. RBAC assigns permissions based on predefined user roles, ensuring that employees, contractors, and partners receive only the necessary access privileges. ABAC extends access control by evaluating user attributes, such as department, job function, and device trust level, to dynamically grant or restrict access based on real-time conditions. IDaaS solutions provide policy-based access management, enabling organizations to define access policies that adapt to evolving business requirements.

Identity lifecycle management is another core function of IDaaS, automating user provisioning, deprovisioning, and access certification processes. Traditional IAM systems require manual user onboarding and offboarding, increasing the risk of orphaned accounts and privilege creep. IDaaS solutions integrate with HR systems and directory services to ensure that user accounts are created, updated, and deactivated in real time based on employment status. System for Cross-domain Identity Management (SCIM) enables automated user provisioning and synchronization across cloud applications, ensuring that identity records remain consistent across all services.

Privileged Access Management (PAM) is a critical extension of IDaaS, ensuring that administrative accounts and high-risk identities are protected from unauthorized access. Traditional IAM models often fail to adequately secure privileged accounts, exposing enterprises to insider threats and credential-based attacks. IDaaS platforms provide Just-In-Time (JIT) privileged access, allowing administrators to request temporary access with time-bound permissions that automatically expire after a predefined period. By integrating PAM with IDaaS, organizations can enforce least privilege access principles, ensuring that privileged actions are logged, monitored, and subject to approval workflows.

Zero Trust security models align with IDaaS by enforcing continuous identity verification and dynamic access control. Unlike traditional perimeter-based security, which assumes trust within corporate networks, Zero Trust IAM continuously evaluates user and device risk before granting access. IDaaS solutions integrate with endpoint security, identity analytics, and threat intelligence to apply real-time risk-based authentication policies. If an identity exhibits suspicious behavior, such as logging in from an unusual location or using a compromised device, IDaaS can enforce additional authentication measures, restrict access, or trigger security alerts.

Compliance and regulatory requirements drive enterprises to adopt IDaaS solutions that support audit logging, access certification, and compliance reporting. Many industries, including finance, healthcare, and government, require strict identity governance to comply with regulations such as GDPR, HIPAA, PCI-DSS, and SOX. IDaaS platforms provide built-in compliance controls, including automated access reviews, policy enforcement, and detailed audit logs of authentication and access activities. Security Information and Event Management (SIEM) integration enables organizations to correlate IAM events with broader security incidents, ensuring continuous compliance monitoring.

API security and machine identity management are essential considerations in IDaaS architectures. Modern applications rely on API-driven interactions, requiring secure API authentication and authorization mechanisms. IDaaS solutions enforce API security through OAuth2 client credentials flow, API key management, and mutual TLS (mTLS) authentication. Machine identities, including service accounts, bots, and automated workflows, require strong identity governance to prevent unauthorized API access. By integrating IDaaS with API gateways and workload identity federation, organizations can enforce secure API access policies while maintaining centralized identity governance.

IAM observability and analytics enhance IDaaS security by providing real-time visibility into authentication patterns, access trends, and identity-related threats. Organizations must implement IAM analytics dashboards, anomaly detection models, and threat intelligence feeds to detect suspicious authentication behaviors. User and Entity Behavior Analytics (UEBA) enhances IDaaS security by identifying deviations from normal access patterns, enabling proactive threat mitigation. Automated incident response workflows, powered by Security Orchestration, Automation, and Response (SOAR) platforms, allow security teams to quickly respond to IAM security incidents, reducing risk exposure.

Scalability and performance optimization are critical for IDaaS in large enterprises, ensuring that identity services remain highly available and responsive under heavy authentication loads. IDaaS providers leverage globally distributed identity services, load balancing, and caching mechanisms to handle millions of authentication requests with low latency. Edge-based authentication proxies, Content Delivery Networks (CDNs), and regional IAM deployments further enhance performance, ensuring seamless user experiences across geographically dispersed enterprise environments.

Enterprises adopting IDaaS must carefully evaluate vendor capabilities, integration flexibility, and security controls to ensure alignment with business requirements. While IDaaS simplifies IAM management, organizations must ensure that identity policies, data residency, and encryption mechanisms comply with corporate security mandates. Hybrid IAM architectures, combining IDaaS with on-premises identity providers, provide a balanced approach for enterprises transitioning to cloud-based IAM while maintaining control over legacy identity systems.

By architecting IDaaS solutions that integrate authentication, authorization, threat intelligence, and compliance, enterprises can achieve scalable, secure, and policy-driven IAM frameworks. IDaaS enhances security by enforcing Zero Trust principles, automating identity lifecycle management, and providing real-time identity analytics. As digital transformation accelerates, enterprises must leverage IDaaS to strengthen identity security, streamline access management, and ensure adaptive IAM policies that support evolving business needs.

IAM and DevSecOps: Embedding Identity Security into CI/CD Pipelines

Identity and Access Management (IAM) has traditionally been viewed as a security layer applied after application development, but in modern DevSecOps environments, IAM must be embedded directly into Continuous Integration and Continuous Deployment (CI/CD) pipelines. As enterprises accelerate software development and automate deployments, the need for robust identity security within DevSecOps workflows becomes critical. IAM in DevSecOps ensures that developers, automated processes, and application components follow least privilege principles, secure authentication mechanisms, and fine-grained access controls at every stage of the software development lifecycle (SDLC). By integrating IAM with CI/CD pipelines, organizations can enforce security policies, reduce identity-based attack surfaces, and prevent unauthorized access to sensitive code repositories, build environments, and production deployments.

The shift-left security philosophy in DevSecOps emphasizes integrating IAM controls early in the development process rather than treating identity security as an afterthought. In traditional IT environments, IAM policies are enforced during application deployment, often requiring security teams to manually configure access controls, define roles, and validate permissions post-deployment. However, in modern DevSecOps workflows, identity security must be codified as part of Infrastructure as Code (IaC), ensuring that access controls are defined, versioned, and enforced programmatically. By embedding IAM policies directly into CI/CD pipelines, organizations reduce the risk of misconfigurations, privilege escalations, and unauthorized access during the software delivery process.

One of the key IAM challenges in DevSecOps is securing developer and machine identities across development, testing, staging, and production environments. Developers often require access to source code repositories, cloud infrastructure, and CI/CD tools, but granting persistent credentials increases security risks. Organizations must implement Just-In-Time (JIT) access provisioning, where developer credentials are issued dynamically for specific tasks and revoked immediately after use. This approach prevents long-lived credentials from being exposed in code repositories or exploited by malicious actors. Temporary access tokens, role-based access control (RBAC), and Attribute-Based Access Control (ABAC) further restrict developer permissions based on predefined security policies.

Machine identities play a crucial role in CI/CD pipelines, as automated build systems, deployment scripts, and container orchestration platforms require authentication to access repositories, package registries, and cloud services. Hardcoded API keys and long-lived access tokens are common security risks in DevSecOps environments, making them a prime target for attackers. Organizations must implement workload identity federation, allowing CI/CD processes to authenticate securely without relying on static credentials. Cloud-native identity solutions such as AWS IAM Roles for Service Accounts (IRSA), Azure Managed Identities, and Google Workload Identity Federation enable CI/CD pipelines to authenticate dynamically using short-lived credentials.

Secrets management is another critical aspect of IAM in DevSecOps, ensuring that sensitive credentials, encryption keys, and authentication tokens are stored securely. Many security breaches occur due to secrets being embedded in source code, CI/CD configuration files, or container images. DevSecOps teams must integrate IAM with secrets management solutions such as HashiCorp Vault, AWS Secrets Manager, and Azure Key Vault to securely store and retrieve secrets during build and deployment processes. Role-based access policies should be enforced to ensure that only authorized processes and identities can access sensitive secrets, reducing the risk of credential leakage.

IAM automation in CI/CD pipelines enforces security policies at each stage of the development process, preventing misconfigured access controls from reaching production environments. By integrating IAM policy validation into CI/CD workflows, organizations can automatically scan identity configurations, detect excessive privileges, and enforce least privilege principles before code is deployed. Open Policy Agent (OPA), AWS IAM Access Analyzer, and Azure Policy provide automated policy enforcement mechanisms that validate IAM configurations as part of the software build process. Any misconfigured permissions or overprivileged roles can trigger automated pipeline failures, ensuring that insecure IAM policies do not propagate into production.

Multi-factor authentication (MFA) must also be enforced within DevSecOps workflows, particularly for high-risk operations such as code commits, infrastructure modifications, and production deployments. Developers and DevOps engineers should be required to authenticate using MFA when accessing CI/CD tools, cloud consoles, and code repositories. Conditional access policies can enforce MFA dynamically based on risk factors, such as login attempts from untrusted devices, abnormal access patterns, or privileged role escalations. By integrating IAM with risk-based authentication mechanisms, organizations enhance identity security without disrupting developer productivity.

IAM observability in DevSecOps ensures that identity-related security events are continuously monitored and analyzed for potential threats. Security teams must implement centralized IAM logging, audit trails, and real-time monitoring to track authentication attempts, permission changes, and access anomalies across CI/CD environments. Logs from IAM providers, CI/CD tools, and cloud identity services should be aggregated into Security Information and Event Management (SIEM) platforms such as Splunk, Elastic Security, or Google Chronicle for threat analysis. User and Entity Behavior Analytics (UEBA) further enhances IAM security by detecting unusual identity behaviors, such as unauthorized privilege escalations or abnormal deployment patterns.

Zero Trust principles should be applied to IAM in DevSecOps, ensuring that every identity, whether human or machine, is continuously verified and authenticated before accessing critical infrastructure. Traditional security models often assume implicit trust for developers and automation scripts within CI/CD pipelines, but Zero Trust IAM enforces strict access controls based on identity risk scores, device trust levels, and contextual security signals. By integrating IAM with Zero Trust frameworks, organizations can dynamically enforce least privilege access, preventing compromised credentials from being exploited within development and deployment workflows.

IAM governance in DevSecOps requires periodic access reviews, role recertification, and compliance-driven policy enforcement to ensure that access permissions remain aligned with security best practices. Automated IAM compliance checks should be integrated into CI/CD pipelines, validating that IAM policies comply with regulatory frameworks such as GDPR, HIPAA, PCI-DSS, and NIST 800-53. Security teams should conduct regular IAM audits to identify inactive accounts, excessive permissions, and role misconfigurations, reducing the risk of privilege creep in CI/CD environments.

By embedding IAM into DevSecOps pipelines, organizations achieve a secure and scalable approach to identity management, reducing attack surfaces while maintaining development velocity. Automating IAM policy enforcement, securing developer and machine identities, and integrating IAM observability into CI/CD workflows ensure that identity security remains a core component of software delivery. As organizations continue to adopt cloud-native development and microservices architectures, IAM must evolve alongside DevSecOps practices to provide dynamic, adaptive, and policy-driven identity security at every stage of the software development lifecycle.

IAM and Software Supply Chain Security: Architecting Trust Across Dependencies

Identity and Access Management (IAM) is a critical component of securing the software supply chain, ensuring that only trusted entities—whether users, machines, or automated workflows—can interact with development, build, and deployment environments. As software ecosystems grow more interconnected, the security of a single organization is no longer sufficient; enterprises must extend trust and identity controls across dependencies, third-party vendors, and open-source software components. Recent high-profile software supply chain attacks, such as SolarWinds and CodeCov, have demonstrated the need for robust identity governance, least privilege access, and continuous authentication within the software development lifecycle (SDLC). By integrating IAM into software supply chain security, organizations can prevent unauthorized code modifications, mitigate dependency risks, and enforce verifiable trust across all components of the development pipeline.

The software supply chain consists of multiple interconnected layers, including source code repositories, third-party libraries, package registries, build systems, CI/CD pipelines, and cloud deployment platforms. Each of these components represents a potential attack vector where adversaries can exploit weak identity controls to inject malicious code, compromise sensitive credentials, or manipulate build artifacts. Traditional IAM models that focus solely on user authentication are insufficient in securing the modern software supply chain, where machine identities, API integrations, and automation play an equally critical role. Organizations must adopt a holistic IAM approach that enforces strict authentication, authorization, and identity auditing across every dependency and software artifact.

One of the primary IAM challenges in software supply chain security is securing developer identities and access to source code repositories. Developers often require elevated access to modify code, manage dependencies, and interact with CI/CD systems. However, persistent administrative privileges increase the risk of insider threats and credential-based attacks. Organizations must enforce least privilege access (LPA) and Just-In-Time (JIT) permissions, ensuring that developers receive only the necessary access rights for specific tasks and for a limited duration. Role-Based Access Control (RBAC) and Attribute-Based Access Control (ABAC) policies should be applied to restrict access based on project requirements, reducing the likelihood of unauthorized code modifications.

Machine identities are equally critical in securing the software supply chain, as automated processes—such as CI/CD pipelines, container orchestration, and deployment scripts—require authentication to interact with repositories, artifact registries, and cloud services. Hardcoded API keys, long-lived access tokens, and unsecured service accounts are common vulnerabilities that attackers exploit to gain unauthorized access to build systems. To mitigate these risks, organizations should implement workload identity federation, leveraging cloud-native identity solutions such as AWS IAM Roles for Service Accounts (IRSA), Azure Managed Identities, and Google Workload Identity Federation. These solutions allow CI/CD workloads to authenticate securely without exposing static credentials, ensuring that machine identities are dynamically verified before accessing critical infrastructure.

Another key aspect of IAM in software supply chain security is enforcing integrity verification for third-party dependencies. Modern software applications rely heavily on open-source libraries, container images, and external package managers such as npm, PyPI, Maven, and Docker Hub. Attackers frequently target these dependencies by injecting malicious code into widely used packages, compromising thousands of downstream applications. IAM solutions must integrate with software composition analysis (SCA) tools and cryptographic signing mechanisms to verify the authenticity of dependencies before they are included in builds. Code signing with digital certificates, such as those issued by Sigstore or Notary, ensures that only trusted, unmodified packages are allowed in production environments.

IAM policy enforcement should extend to CI/CD pipelines, preventing unauthorized code changes, insecure build configurations, and privilege escalation attempts. CI/CD platforms such as GitHub Actions, GitLab CI, Jenkins, and Azure DevOps must be configured with strong authentication controls, including enforced multi-factor authentication (MFA) for developers, signed commit verification, and automated IAM policy validation. Integrating IAM with CI/CD pipelines allows organizations to enforce security gates that validate identity attributes before approving deployments. For example, a CI/CD job attempting to push a container image to a production registry should only be allowed if the request originates from an authenticated pipeline execution with a verified commit signature.

IAM observability and real-time threat detection play a crucial role in securing the software supply chain. Organizations must implement centralized identity monitoring to track authentication attempts, access requests, and permission changes across all supply chain components. Security Information and Event Management (SIEM) platforms should aggregate IAM logs from repositories, build systems, and package registries, correlating identity events with broader security incidents. User and Entity Behavior Analytics (UEBA) further enhances IAM security by detecting anomalies such as unusual commit patterns, excessive privilege escalations, or unauthorized API calls.

Automated incident response workflows, powered by Security Orchestration, Automation, and Response (SOAR) platforms, can revoke credentials, disable compromised accounts, and trigger security audits in response to detected threats.

Zero Trust IAM principles must be applied to software supply chain security, ensuring that every identity—human or machine—is continuously verified and authorized before interacting with development and deployment environments. Traditional perimeter-based security models, which assume implicit trust for internal entities, are inadequate for modern software supply chains, where dependencies span multiple organizations and cloud environments. By implementing Zero Trust IAM, organizations enforce continuous authentication, risk-based access controls, and policy-driven security enforcement across all software development stages.

Regulatory compliance and IAM governance are essential in software supply chain security, as many industries require strict access controls, auditability, and software integrity verification. Regulations such as GDPR, HIPAA, PCI-DSS, and NIST 800-218 (Secure Software Development Framework) mandate that organizations implement secure software development practices, enforce IAM controls, and maintain audit logs of code changes and access permissions. IAM solutions must integrate with compliance automation tools, ensuring that identity policies, role assignments, and software artifacts comply with industry standards. Automated access reviews and policy enforcement mechanisms further ensure that IAM configurations remain secure and aligned with compliance requirements.

Future-proofing IAM for software supply chain security requires continuous adaptation to emerging threats, integration with next-generation security technologies, and the adoption of identity-centric security frameworks. Organizations must invest in AI-driven IAM analytics that detect supply chain attacks in real time, blockchain-based identity verification for software artifacts, and decentralized identity models that reduce reliance on centralized IAM providers. As the complexity of software supply chains increases, IAM must evolve to provide real-time trust validation, automated security policy enforcement, and seamless identity federation across all dependencies.

By embedding IAM into software supply chain security, organizations establish a verifiable trust framework that protects software development, build environments, and deployment processes from identity-based threats. Implementing least privilege access, securing machine identities, enforcing cryptographic signing for dependencies, and integrating IAM observability ensures that software artifacts remain secure, authenticated, and tamper-proof. As supply chain attacks continue to rise, organizations must prioritize IAM as a foundational security measure, safeguarding both proprietary and open-source software ecosystems against unauthorized modifications, credential theft, and dependency compromise.

Architecting Privacy-Preserving IAM Solutions: Zero-Knowledge Proofs and Differential Privacy

Identity and Access Management (IAM) traditionally focuses on securing authentication and authorization while ensuring compliance with regulatory frameworks. However, as data privacy concerns grow, organizations must implement IAM solutions that not only verify identities but also minimize exposure of personally identifiable information (PII). Privacy-preserving IAM architectures leverage cryptographic techniques such as Zero-Knowledge Proofs (ZKPs) and Differential Privacy (DP) to authenticate users, enforce access controls, and analyze identity data without exposing sensitive information. By integrating these techniques into IAM frameworks, organizations can enhance security, comply with data protection regulations, and provide users with greater control over their digital identities.

Zero-Knowledge Proofs (ZKPs) enable identity verification without revealing underlying credentials or sensitive attributes. Traditional authentication methods require users to disclose information such as passwords, biometric data, or government-issued identifiers to prove their identity. This exposes user data to potential leaks, breaches, and surveillance. ZKPs allow users to authenticate by proving that they possess valid credentials without disclosing the credentials themselves.

This cryptographic method ensures that identity verification is performed in a privacy-preserving manner, preventing unauthorized entities from collecting or storing unnecessary user data.

One of the most common applications of ZKPs in IAM is in passwordless authentication. Instead of sending a password or a one-time code to a server, a user can generate a cryptographic proof that they know a secret without revealing the secret itself. For example, a Zero-Knowledge Succinct Non-Interactive Argument of Knowledge (zk-SNARK) can be used to prove that a user has access to a private key associated with their identity without transmitting the private key. This prevents credential replay attacks, phishing attempts, and unauthorized access based on leaked credentials.

ZKPs also improve identity federation and Single Sign-On (SSO) by eliminating the need for third-party identity providers to store or transmit identity attributes. In traditional federated authentication models, identity providers (IdPs) issue security tokens containing user attributes, which are then verified by service providers (SPs). This model creates a central trust authority that may collect, track, and analyze user behavior. With ZKPs, identity verification can occur in a decentralized manner, allowing users to prove their eligibility for services without exposing personal details. This is particularly beneficial in privacy-sensitive industries such as finance, healthcare, and government services.

Another critical aspect of privacy-preserving IAM is enforcing access control while minimizing data exposure. Traditional access control mechanisms rely on explicit identity attributes, such as user roles, job titles, or access levels, which must be shared with access control systems. Using ZKPs, users can prove they meet certain access criteria without revealing specific attributes. For example, a user could prove they are over 18 without disclosing their exact birthdate, or a researcher could verify that they belong to an accredited institution without revealing their employer's name. This fine-grained access control enhances privacy while maintaining strong security.

Differential Privacy (DP) complements ZKPs by ensuring that statistical data derived from IAM systems does not expose individual identities. Organizations often analyze authentication logs, access patterns, and behavioral analytics to detect security threats and improve IAM policies. However, collecting and analyzing this data can introduce privacy risks, particularly when IAM logs contain detailed user activities. Differential Privacy techniques introduce carefully calibrated noise into datasets, allowing organizations to gain insights while preventing re-identification of individual users.

One of the primary applications of DP in IAM is in anomaly detection and risk-based authentication. IAM systems continuously monitor login attempts, privilege escalations, and access requests to detect unusual behavior that may indicate account compromise or insider threats. By applying DP techniques, IAM systems can analyze aggregate trends without exposing specific user behaviors. For example, an IAM system could detect an increase in suspicious logins from a particular country without revealing which users are affected. This ensures that privacy is maintained while enabling proactive security measures.

DP is also useful for compliance reporting and auditing in IAM. Many regulatory frameworks, such as GDPR, HIPAA, and CCPA, require organizations to perform security audits and generate reports on IAM activities. However, sharing raw authentication logs with auditors, third-party vendors, or regulators may violate user privacy. By applying DP algorithms, organizations can generate statistical reports that demonstrate compliance without disclosing individual user identities. This approach balances transparency with data protection, ensuring that organizations meet regulatory requirements while safeguarding user privacy.

IAM solutions incorporating privacy-preserving techniques must also address identity governance and consent management. Users should have control over how their identity data is shared, used, and stored. Decentralized identity frameworks, such as Self-Sovereign Identity (SSI), integrate well with ZKPs and DP by enabling users to generate verifiable credentials that disclose only the necessary information. In a privacy-preserving IAM system, users can specify which attributes they want to share with applications while maintaining anonymity for unrelated data points. This allows for greater user autonomy and minimizes the risk of data misuse.

Implementing privacy-preserving IAM solutions requires integrating ZKP and DP techniques into existing authentication protocols, access control mechanisms, and identity analytics workflows. Standard IAM technologies such as OAuth2, OpenID Connect (OIDC), and SAML can be extended with ZKP-based authentication methods, allowing for privacy-preserving login experiences. Similarly, IAM logging systems can incorporate DP techniques to anonymize audit trails while maintaining security insights. Organizations should also consider integrating privacy-enhancing cryptographic libraries, such as zk-SNARKs for authentication proofs and DP frameworks for IAM analytics.

Scalability and performance optimization are key considerations when deploying privacy-preserving IAM solutions. ZKPs, particularly in zero-trust authentication workflows, require computational resources to generate and verify cryptographic proofs. While zk-SNARKs and zk-STARKs provide efficient proof generation, organizations must ensure that IAM infrastructure can handle real-time authentication requests without introducing excessive latency. Similarly, DP implementations must balance privacy guarantees with data utility, ensuring that IAM analytics remain actionable without excessive noise.

Future developments in privacy-preserving IAM will focus on enhancing usability, interoperability, and standardization. Emerging cryptographic techniques, such as Fully Homomorphic Encryption (FHE) and Secure Multi-Party Computation (SMPC), will further enable privacy-preserving IAM architectures that minimize data exposure during authentication and access control operations. Additionally, industry-wide initiatives, such as the World Wide Web Consortium (W3C) Verifiable Credentials standard, will continue to drive adoption of privacy-enhancing identity technologies.

By integrating Zero-Knowledge Proofs and Differential Privacy into IAM architectures, organizations can enhance identity security while protecting user privacy. These techniques enable authentication, access control, and identity analytics without exposing sensitive information, ensuring compliance with global data protection regulations. Privacy-preserving IAM solutions provide users with greater control over their digital identities while reducing the risks of data breaches, surveillance, and identity theft. As organizations move towards more privacy-centric IAM frameworks, adopting ZKP and DP will be essential in building trust, security, and regulatory compliance in identity management ecosystems.

IAM and Blockchain: Architecting Distributed Identity Verification Frameworks

Identity and Access Management (IAM) has traditionally relied on centralized identity providers to authenticate and authorize users. However, centralized IAM systems introduce security risks, data privacy concerns, and a single point of failure. Blockchain technology offers an alternative approach to identity verification by enabling decentralized identity frameworks that provide security, transparency, and user control. By integrating blockchain into IAM, organizations can create distributed identity verification frameworks that enhance trust, reduce reliance on central authorities, and improve interoperability across multiple platforms and organizations.

Blockchain-based IAM solutions leverage decentralized ledger technology (DLT) to store and verify identity credentials without relying on a single trusted authority. Unlike traditional IAM models where identity data is managed by enterprises or identity providers (IdPs), blockchain allows identities to be self-sovereign, meaning users retain control over their credentials. In a decentralized IAM framework, identity attributes are stored as verifiable credentials on a blockchain, enabling users to authenticate with service providers without exposing sensitive personal data. This model enhances privacy and security while ensuring that identity verification processes remain tamper-proof.

Self-Sovereign Identity (SSI) is a key concept in blockchain-based IAM, allowing individuals and organizations to create, manage, and share their digital identities without dependence on centralized entities. SSI frameworks use decentralized identifiers (DIDs), cryptographic signatures, and verifiable credentials to authenticate users securely.

When a user needs to prove their identity, they provide a cryptographic proof instead of revealing raw identity data. For example, a user applying for a loan could prove they are over 18 without disclosing their birthdate, or an employee could verify their job title without revealing other employment details.

Verifiable credentials in blockchain IAM systems ensure trust while minimizing identity exposure. Traditional identity verification processes require users to share personally identifiable information (PII) with multiple service providers, increasing the risk of data breaches and identity theft. Blockchain-based verifiable credentials allow users to share cryptographic proofs that confirm the authenticity of their claims without revealing unnecessary details. These credentials are issued by trusted institutions, such as governments, universities, or financial institutions, and stored in a user-controlled digital wallet. Service providers can verify these credentials against the blockchain without needing direct access to the issuer's data.

Interoperability is a significant advantage of blockchain IAM frameworks, enabling seamless identity verification across different platforms, industries, and jurisdictions. Traditional IAM systems often struggle with cross-platform authentication due to differences in identity providers, authentication protocols, and regulatory requirements. Blockchain-based identity frameworks use open standards, such as the W3C Verifiable Credentials (VC) standard and Decentralized Identifier (DID) specifications, to ensure compatibility across multiple identity ecosystems. This interoperability allows users to authenticate across government services, financial institutions, and online platforms without needing multiple credentials.

Security and fraud prevention are strengthened in blockchain-based IAM by leveraging cryptographic techniques and distributed consensus mechanisms. In centralized IAM systems, identity records are vulnerable to breaches if the identity provider is compromised. Blockchain mitigates this risk by distributing identity verification records across multiple nodes, ensuring that no single entity can alter or falsify identity data. Smart contracts can automate identity validation processes, reducing the risk of social engineering attacks and credential misuse. By enforcing cryptographic trust mechanisms, blockchain-based IAM minimizes identity fraud while maintaining decentralized security guarantees.

Zero-Knowledge Proofs (ZKPs) enhance privacy in blockchain IAM by allowing users to prove identity attributes without revealing underlying data. Traditional authentication methods require users to disclose personal information, increasing exposure to potential data breaches. With ZKPs, users can prove eligibility for services, such as proving citizenship or employment status, without sharing sensitive details. Blockchain IAM frameworks integrate ZKPs to enforce selective disclosure, ensuring that users retain control over their data while meeting authentication requirements.

Decentralized access control mechanisms in blockchain-based IAM enable fine-grained authorization policies without relying on central administrators. Traditional IAM systems use Role-Based Access Control (RBAC) and Attribute-Based Access Control (ABAC) to grant permissions, but these models require centralized policy enforcement. Blockchain IAM introduces decentralized access control through smart contracts, where access permissions are enforced through cryptographic rules stored on the blockchain. For example, an organization could define a policy that automatically grants access to certain documents if a user's verifiable credentials match predefined criteria. This approach eliminates the need for manual access approvals, reducing administrative overhead while ensuring secure and automated access control.

Blockchain-based IAM solutions also enhance identity recovery and resilience. In traditional IAM systems, recovering lost credentials often requires interacting with a central authority, creating a dependency on the identity provider. Decentralized identity recovery models use multi-signature authentication, social recovery mechanisms, and decentralized key management to enable users to regain access to their identities without relying on a single recovery authority. For example, a user could designate trusted contacts or multiple authentication factors to recover their identity in case of credential loss. This decentralized approach enhances security and ensures that users retain control over their digital identities.

Regulatory compliance is an important consideration when implementing blockchain IAM frameworks. Privacy laws such as GDPR, CCPA, and HIPAA impose strict requirements on how identity data is collected, stored, and processed. Blockchain IAM solutions must incorporate privacy-preserving techniques, such as data minimization, selective disclosure, and off-chain storage, to ensure compliance with regulatory mandates. While blockchain provides immutable identity verification records, sensitive PII should be stored off-chain with access controls managed through verifiable credentials. This hybrid approach balances the transparency and security benefits of blockchain with regulatory privacy requirements.

Scalability and performance are challenges in blockchain-based IAM due to the computational overhead of cryptographic operations and decentralized consensus mechanisms. Public blockchains, such as Ethereum and Bitcoin, face scalability limitations that may impact real-time authentication processes. To address these challenges, IAM frameworks leverage layer-2 scaling solutions, such as sidechains and state channels, to reduce transaction latency while maintaining decentralized security guarantees. Hybrid blockchain models, where identity verification occurs on permissioned blockchains while public blockchains serve as trust anchors, further improve scalability without compromising security.

Enterprise adoption of blockchain IAM is increasing, particularly in industries that require high-assurance identity verification, such as finance, healthcare, and supply chain management. Financial institutions use blockchain IAM for Know Your Customer (KYC) compliance, enabling seamless identity verification across banks and payment networks. Healthcare organizations implement decentralized identity frameworks to protect patient records while allowing secure access to medical data across multiple providers. In supply chain security, blockchain IAM ensures that only verified entities can access logistics systems, preventing fraudulent transactions and counterfeiting.

The future of blockchain IAM will involve deeper integration with decentralized finance (DeFi), Web3 applications, and digital identity ecosystems. As blockchain technology continues to evolve, identity verification frameworks will become more efficient, scalable, and user-friendly. Emerging identity standards, such as Self-Sovereign Identity (SSI) and Decentralized Identity (DID), will drive greater adoption of blockchain-based IAM solutions, enabling individuals and organizations to manage identities securely in a trustless environment.

By architecting blockchain-based IAM frameworks, organizations can enhance security, privacy, and interoperability while reducing reliance on centralized identity providers. The decentralized nature of blockchain IAM ensures that identity verification remains tamper-proof, privacy-preserving, and resilient against fraud. As digital transformation accelerates, blockchain IAM will play a pivotal role in enabling trusted, scalable, and secure identity verification across industries and global ecosystems.

Designing IAM for Autonomous Systems, AI Agents, and Self-Healing Networks

Identity and Access Management (IAM) has traditionally been designed for human users, applications, and networked services. However, the rise of autonomous systems, artificial intelligence (AI) agents, and self-healing networks introduces new identity challenges that require adaptive, context-aware IAM architectures. Unlike conventional identity models, where authentication and authorization are assigned to static entities, autonomous systems operate dynamically, making real-time decisions, adapting to changes, and interacting with other intelligent entities. IAM must evolve to accommodate AI-driven identities, enforce fine-grained access controls, and ensure security without human intervention.

Autonomous systems, such as self-driving vehicles, industrial robots, and unmanned aerial vehicles (UAVs), require machine identities that enable them to authenticate, authorize, and interact with cloud platforms, sensors, and external services. Unlike traditional IAM models where users log in and assume predefined roles, autonomous entities must establish their own credentials, request access dynamically, and revoke privileges when no longer needed. This requires IAM solutions to support identity federation across distributed AI ecosystems, ensuring that autonomous systems can securely interact without manual oversight.

Machine identities must be secured using cryptographic techniques such as Public Key Infrastructure (PKI), mutual TLS (mTLS), and token-based authentication. Instead of relying on static credentials, IAM solutions should implement ephemeral identity tokens that expire after short durations, preventing unauthorized use. AI agents operating in dynamic environments must generate, validate, and renew their credentials autonomously, ensuring continuous authentication without human intervention. These identity mechanisms prevent credential misuse and unauthorized privilege escalation in AI-driven systems.

AI agents, such as intelligent chatbots, automated cybersecurity responders, and robotic process automation (RPA) systems, require adaptive IAM policies that define identity attributes based on contextual behavior. Unlike human users, whose identities remain relatively static, AI agents evolve based on training data, learned behaviors, and operational tasks. IAM frameworks must integrate behavioral analytics and risk-based authentication to continuously evaluate AI-driven identities, detecting anomalies that may indicate compromised AI models or adversarial manipulation. If an AI agent suddenly requests access to unauthorized resources, IAM policies should enforce step-up authentication, revoke privileges, or trigger security audits.

Self-healing networks, powered by AI-driven orchestration, introduce additional IAM complexity by autonomously modifying network configurations, deploying security patches, and responding to cyber threats in real time. Traditional IAM frameworks rely on predefined access control policies, but self-healing networks require dynamic IAM enforcement that adapts based on network conditions, threat intelligence, and anomaly detection. IAM solutions should leverage Policy-Based Access Control (PBAC) and Attribute-Based Access Control (ABAC) to enable context-aware decision-making for autonomous remediation actions.

Zero Trust principles must be embedded into IAM architectures for autonomous systems to ensure that every AI-driven entity continuously authenticates and revalidates its identity before executing critical operations. Unlike legacy perimeter-based security models, where trusted entities retain persistent access, Zero Trust IAM enforces just-in-time (JIT) authentication, requiring AI agents and self-healing networks to verify their identity before initiating changes. This approach prevents unauthorized AI models from gaining control over sensitive infrastructure and ensures that self-healing actions are authenticated before modifying security configurations.

Machine-to-machine (M2M) authentication is a critical aspect of IAM for autonomous systems, ensuring that AI agents and self-healing networks can communicate securely across distributed environments. IAM solutions should enforce mTLS authentication, OAuth2-based service-to-service authentication, and federated identity mechanisms that allow AI agents to authenticate across cloud, edge, and on-premises environments. Federated identity architectures ensure that autonomous entities can authenticate using decentralized credentials while enforcing access control policies that prevent unauthorized cross-domain interactions.

IAM for AI-driven systems must also address identity lifecycle management, ensuring that machine identities are provisioned, updated, and decommissioned as AI models evolve. Unlike human users, who follow traditional identity lifecycle processes, AI agents require dynamic identity governance that adapts based on operational tasks, security posture, and contextual risk factors. IAM frameworks should implement AI-driven identity governance solutions that automatically adjust permissions, revoke access when AI agents become inactive, and enforce role reassignment based on learned behaviors.

Anomaly detection and threat intelligence must be integrated into IAM frameworks to identify malicious AI behavior and prevent adversarial attacks. AI-driven IAM analytics should continuously monitor authentication logs, API calls, and network interactions to detect unauthorized privilege escalations, AI model tampering, and synthetic identity attacks. If an AI agent begins exhibiting behavior inconsistent with its historical patterns—such as requesting access to high-privilege accounts or modifying security policies—IAM solutions should enforce automated response actions, including revoking credentials, sandboxing AI agents, or triggering forensic investigations.

IAM for autonomous systems must also incorporate explainability and transparency mechanisms to ensure that AI-driven identity decisions can be audited and verified. Unlike traditional IAM policies, which rely on human-defined rules, AI-driven IAM policies may evolve autonomously based on learned data. Organizations must implement AI explainability frameworks that allow security teams to understand why AI agents are granted specific privileges, ensuring that identity policies remain auditable and compliant with regulatory requirements.

Regulatory compliance introduces additional IAM challenges for AI-driven identities, as industries such as finance, healthcare, and defense require strict access controls for autonomous systems. IAM frameworks must enforce policy-driven compliance mechanisms that ensure AI-driven authentication and access control decisions align with industry regulations such as GDPR, HIPAA, and ISO 27001. AI-driven IAM solutions should implement cryptographic auditing, ensuring that identity logs remain tamper-proof while enabling real-time compliance reporting.

The future of IAM for autonomous systems will involve deeper integration with decentralized identity frameworks, blockchain-based identity verification, and AI-driven IAM automation. Decentralized identity standards, such as Self-Sovereign Identity (SSI) and Decentralized Identifiers (DIDs), will enable AI agents and self-healing networks to authenticate without relying on centralized identity providers. Blockchain-based IAM solutions will provide verifiable identity proofs, ensuring that AI-driven entities can establish trust without exposing sensitive identity attributes.

By designing IAM solutions for autonomous systems, AI agents, and self-healing networks, organizations create a resilient, adaptive, and AI-aware security architecture that enforces identity trust, dynamic access control, and real-time threat detection. As AI-driven systems continue to evolve, IAM must advance to provide scalable, privacy-preserving, and continuously adaptive identity solutions that support autonomous decision-making while preventing unauthorized access and adversarial manipulation.

IAM for Financial Services: Architecting Identity for High-Security Banking Systems

Identity and Access Management (IAM) in financial services plays a crucial role in protecting sensitive customer data, securing banking transactions, and ensuring compliance with strict regulatory frameworks. Unlike traditional IAM implementations, identity security in banking environments requires enhanced authentication mechanisms, real-time fraud detection, and dynamic access control policies that mitigate risks associated with insider threats, cyberattacks, and account takeovers. Financial institutions must architect IAM solutions that balance security, usability, and regulatory compliance while enabling seamless access to banking services across digital channels.

High-security banking systems demand multi-layered authentication mechanisms to prevent unauthorized access to financial accounts and transactional data. Traditional username-password authentication models are insufficient for financial services due to the risk of credential theft, phishing attacks, and brute-force exploits. Multi-Factor Authentication (MFA) is a mandatory security control for banking IAM, requiring users to authenticate using multiple factors such as biometrics, hardware security keys, or mobile-based authentication codes. Adaptive authentication further enhances security by analyzing contextual risk factors, such as device fingerprinting, geolocation, and transaction anomalies, before granting access. If a high-risk authentication attempt is detected, IAM systems can enforce step-up authentication, requiring additional verification before proceeding.

Privileged Access Management (PAM) is a critical component of IAM in financial services, ensuring that administrative accounts, database operators, and security analysts have controlled and monitored access to sensitive banking infrastructure. Financial institutions must implement Just-In-Time (JIT) access provisioning for privileged users, granting temporary elevated permissions only when necessary and revoking them immediately after use. Role-Based Access Control

(RBAC) and Attribute-Based Access Control (ABAC) must be enforced to ensure that privileged accounts operate under the principle of least privilege, preventing unauthorized access to core banking applications, customer account data, and financial transaction records.

Identity federation and Single Sign-On (SSO) are essential for securing banking ecosystems that integrate with multiple third-party services, cloud applications, and regulatory platforms. Financial institutions often operate within a complex identity landscape, where users authenticate across multiple banking applications, payment networks, and compliance portals. Implementing federated identity management using SAML, OpenID Connect (OIDC), and OAuth2 enables seamless authentication across banking platforms while reducing password fatigue and minimizing credential reuse. Federated identity also supports secure customer authentication in open banking ecosystems, allowing third-party financial service providers to authenticate users through bank-issued identity credentials.

Real-time fraud detection and anomaly detection must be integrated into IAM for banking systems, ensuring that identity-related threats are identified and mitigated before financial losses occur. User and Entity Behavior Analytics (UEBA) enhances IAM security by monitoring authentication patterns, transactional behavior, and privileged access requests to detect suspicious activity. If an IAM system identifies deviations from normal banking behavior—such as rapid fund transfers, unusual login locations, or unauthorized privilege escalations—it can trigger automated responses, such as account lockout, transaction review, or immediate identity re-verification.

Zero Trust security models align closely with IAM in financial services, enforcing continuous identity verification and least privilege access at every stage of a banking session. Unlike traditional perimeter-based security, which assumes internal users are inherently trusted, Zero Trust IAM ensures that all access requests—whether from employees, customers, or third-party service providers—are continuously validated based on identity risk scores, contextual factors, and behavioral analytics. Implementing Zero Trust IAM in banking environments reduces the risk of credential compromise, insider fraud, and unauthorized API access.

API security is another critical IAM consideration in financial services, as modern banking systems rely on APIs for account management, transaction processing, and third-party service integrations. Open banking initiatives, such as PSD2 in Europe, require banks to expose APIs to third-party financial service providers while ensuring strong identity verification and access control enforcement. IAM solutions must enforce OAuth2-based API authentication, API rate limiting, and mutual TLS (mTLS) authentication to prevent unauthorized access to banking APIs. Implementing API gateways with IAM integration ensures that only authorized applications and services can access sensitive financial data.

Identity governance and compliance play a significant role in financial IAM, as banking institutions must adhere to strict regulatory requirements, including GDPR, PCI-DSS, SOX, and FFIEC guidelines. IAM solutions must support automated access certification, periodic access reviews, and real-time compliance monitoring to ensure that identity policies align with regulatory mandates. Security teams must implement continuous auditing of identity-related events, maintaining detailed logs of authentication attempts, role assignments, and access policy changes to support regulatory investigations and forensic analysis.

Biometric authentication is increasingly being adopted in financial services to provide frictionless yet secure user authentication. Banks and financial institutions leverage fingerprint recognition, facial biometrics, and voice authentication to enhance security while improving user experience. Biometric IAM solutions must ensure secure storage and encryption of biometric data, preventing unauthorized access and biometric spoofing attacks. Privacy-preserving authentication techniques, such as homomorphic encryption and zero-knowledge proofs, further enhance security by enabling biometric authentication without exposing raw biometric data to authentication servers.

IAM resilience and disaster recovery are critical for ensuring business continuity in financial services. Banking IAM solutions must be architected with high availability, geo-redundant identity stores, and automated failover mechanisms to prevent authentication disruptions. Financial institutions should implement decentralized IAM models that ensure authentication and access control remain operational even in the event of regional outages or cyber incidents. IAM solutions must integrate with Security Orchestration, Automation, and Response (SOAR) platforms to enable rapid identity recovery, automated credential revocation, and real-time threat containment.

Customer identity protection must be a top priority in financial IAM, ensuring that account holders are safeguarded from identity theft, account takeovers, and phishing attacks. Implementing risk-based authentication, email domain verification (DMARC, DKIM, SPF), and behavioral biometrics strengthens identity protection against fraudulent account access attempts. Banks must also provide secure self-service IAM capabilities, enabling customers to manage their authentication preferences, review access logs, and revoke suspicious login sessions in real time.

As financial services continue to adopt cloud-based banking solutions, IAM solutions must evolve to support hybrid cloud environments, multi-cloud identity federation, and decentralized identity models. Cloud-native IAM platforms, such as Microsoft Entra ID, AWS IAM, and Google Cloud Identity, enable banks to implement scalable identity security solutions that integrate with cloud-based financial applications. Hybrid IAM architectures must ensure that on-premises banking systems and cloud-native financial services operate under a unified identity governance framework, maintaining consistent security policies across all environments.

As cybersecurity threats targeting financial institutions become more sophisticated, IAM must continue evolving to meet emerging identity security challenges. AI-driven identity threat intelligence, blockchain-based digital identity verification, and quantum-resistant authentication mechanisms are shaping the future of IAM in financial services. Banks and financial institutions must invest in IAM architectures that enforce continuous identity validation, adaptive authentication, and machine learning-based fraud prevention to protect customer identities, secure financial transactions, and maintain trust in the digital banking ecosystem.

Strategic IAM Investment Planning: Cost Optimization and Business Value Realization

Identity and Access Management (IAM) is a critical pillar of enterprise security, but it also represents a significant financial investment. Organizations must carefully plan IAM investments to balance cost optimization with business value realization, ensuring that security objectives align with operational efficiency and long-term strategic goals. The complexity of IAM ecosystems—including identity governance, authentication infrastructure, privileged access management (PAM), and identity analytics—requires a structured approach to investment planning. Effective IAM financial planning must consider total cost of ownership (TCO), return on investment (ROI), and risk reduction, while also ensuring compliance with regulatory requirements and supporting digital transformation initiatives.

IAM cost optimization starts with understanding the different cost components involved in deploying and maintaining identity solutions. These costs typically include licensing fees for IAM platforms, cloud subscription models, on-premises infrastructure, workforce training, and ongoing administration. Organizations must assess whether a cloud-based Identity as a Service (IDaaS) model or an on-premises deployment provides the best cost-benefit balance. Cloud-based IAM solutions, such as Microsoft Entra ID, Okta, and Ping Identity, offer predictable operational expenses through subscription pricing, reducing the capital expenditures (CapEx) associated with on-premises hardware and software maintenance. However, for enterprises with strict data sovereignty requirements, on-premises IAM may remain a necessary investment, requiring a hybrid IAM strategy that optimizes both cost and security.

Automation plays a crucial role in IAM cost reduction, minimizing manual identity administration efforts while improving security. Many IAM processes, such as user provisioning, access certification, and role recertification, involve significant operational overhead when performed manually. By leveraging identity lifecycle automation tools, such as System for Cross-domain Identity Management (SCIM) and role mining algorithms, organizations can streamline IAM workflows, reducing administrative workload and associated labor costs. Automating identity governance and administration (IGA) reduces human errors, ensures compliance with access policies, and enables organizations to scale IAM operations without increasing personnel expenses.

A major cost factor in IAM investment planning is the integration of identity services with existing enterprise applications, cloud platforms, and third-party SaaS solutions. Many organizations face hidden costs related to custom IAM integrations, API security implementations, and legacy system compatibility issues. Investing in IAM solutions with pre-built connectors and standards-based interoperability, such as SAML, OAuth2, and OpenID Connect, reduces the cost of integration efforts. Enterprises should also prioritize IAM platforms that support low-code or no-code workflows, allowing security teams to define identity policies without extensive custom development.

IAM cost optimization must also address licensing and user-based pricing models, which can significantly impact the overall budget. Some IAM vendors charge based on the number of active users, while others offer tiered pricing for authentication requests or API calls. Organizations must evaluate their user population—including employees, contractors, partners, and customers—to select a licensing model that aligns with actual usage patterns. For enterprises with fluctuating workforce sizes, adopting a pay-as-you-go IAM model with dynamic scaling capabilities reduces costs by ensuring that IAM expenditures align with actual demand.

Privileged Access Management (PAM) is another critical IAM investment area that requires cost optimization. Traditional PAM solutions often involve expensive licensing fees for privileged session management, password vaulting, and Just-In-Time (JIT) privilege escalation. Organizations should assess whether cloud-native PAM solutions, such as AWS Secrets Manager or Azure Privileged Identity Management (PIM), offer cost-effective alternatives to traditional on-premises PAM solutions. Implementing zero standing privileges (ZSP) reduces the need for long-term privileged account licensing, enabling cost savings while improving security.

Business value realization from IAM investments goes beyond cost reduction, as identity security directly contributes to risk mitigation, operational efficiency, and user experience improvements. Organizations must measure the financial impact of IAM investments by assessing reductions in security incidents, compliance violations, and user friction in authentication workflows. IAM solutions that enhance user productivity—such as Single Sign-On (SSO) and passwordless authentication—reduce IT help desk costs by minimizing password reset requests and account lockouts. Implementing adaptive authentication further improves security while reducing user frustration, enhancing business agility and customer satisfaction.

IAM investments also contribute to compliance cost savings by ensuring that access controls align with regulatory mandates, reducing audit failures and penalties. Many industries require strict access management controls under regulations such as GDPR, HIPAA, PCI-DSS, and SOX. Non-compliance can result in hefty fines, legal repercussions, and reputational damage. Investing in IAM solutions with built-in compliance reporting, real-time access monitoring, and automated audit trail generation significantly reduces the cost of regulatory adherence while improving security posture.

IAM cost-benefit analysis must also consider the financial impact of identity-related security breaches. Cyberattacks targeting identity credentials—such as phishing, credential stuffing, and insider threats—can lead to data breaches, financial losses, and reputational damage. Implementing strong IAM security controls, including Multi-Factor Authentication (MFA), risk-based access policies, and identity analytics, reduces the probability of successful attacks. The financial justification for IAM investment should quantify potential breach costs, demonstrating that proactive identity security measures prevent financial losses that far exceed IAM deployment costs.

IAM investment planning should also align with digital transformation initiatives, ensuring that identity security supports cloud adoption, DevSecOps integration, and modern application architectures. Enterprises migrating to multi-cloud environments must invest in IAM solutions that provide consistent identity governance across AWS, Azure, Google Cloud, and SaaS platforms. Organizations adopting DevSecOps practices must integrate IAM into CI/CD pipelines, enforcing security policies for developers and automated deployment workflows. Investing in IAM solutions that support API security, microservices identity federation, and decentralized identity frameworks enhances business agility while maintaining security.

IAM scalability is another key factor in long-term investment planning, ensuring that identity solutions can accommodate business growth without requiring costly overhauls. Organizations must assess whether their IAM architecture can support an increasing number of users, expanding cloud services, and evolving security requirements. Implementing modular IAM frameworks, microservices-based IAM components, and identity orchestration platforms enables enterprises to scale IAM services dynamically, optimizing costs while maintaining flexibility.

Vendor management and IAM contract negotiations also play a role in cost optimization. Enterprises should evaluate multiple IAM vendors, negotiate enterprise licensing agreements, and assess total cost of ownership (TCO) before committing to long-term IAM contracts. Vendor lock-in risks must be carefully managed by selecting IAM solutions that support open standards and interoperability with third-party security tools. Organizations should also explore open-source IAM alternatives, such as Keycloak and WSO2 Identity Server, for cost-effective IAM implementations that avoid proprietary licensing costs.

Strategic IAM investment planning requires a balanced approach that optimizes costs while maximizing security, compliance, and business enablement. Organizations must assess the financial impact of IAM investments across operational expenses, security risk reduction, regulatory compliance, and user productivity gains. By implementing automation, aligning IAM with digital transformation, and leveraging scalable IAM architectures, enterprises can achieve cost-effective identity security that supports long-term business growth and resilience.

IAM Ethics and Governance: Architecting Ethical and Accountable Identity Systems

Identity and Access Management (IAM) plays a central role in securing digital ecosystems, but beyond its technical implementation, IAM must also be designed with ethical considerations and governance principles in mind. The growing reliance on identity systems for authentication, authorization, and digital trust has introduced new ethical challenges, including data privacy concerns, algorithmic bias, surveillance risks, and the potential for abuse of identity information. Ethical IAM architectures must balance security, user rights, regulatory compliance, and transparency while ensuring that identity systems remain accountable and resistant to misuse.

Ethical IAM design begins with respecting user autonomy and ensuring that individuals have control over their digital identities. Traditional IAM models often require users to share extensive personal information without clear visibility into how their data will be used, stored, or shared. Privacy-enhancing IAM architectures must prioritize data minimization, allowing users to authenticate without exposing unnecessary identity attributes. Self-Sovereign Identity (SSI) frameworks, decentralized identity models, and Zero-Knowledge Proofs (ZKPs) enable individuals to verify credentials while maintaining control over their personal data, reducing the risk of identity exploitation.

Algorithmic bias in IAM systems presents a significant ethical challenge, particularly in identity verification, biometric authentication, and risk-based access control. Many IAM solutions incorporate artificial intelligence (AI) and machine learning (ML) models to detect anomalies, enforce adaptive authentication, and perform fraud detection. However, if these models are trained on biased datasets, they may unfairly disadvantage certain demographics, leading to higher false rejection rates for underrepresented groups. Ethical IAM governance requires organizations to audit and mitigate bias in AI-driven identity systems, ensuring that authentication and authorization decisions are impartial and based on fair and transparent criteria.

Surveillance risks in IAM architectures must also be carefully managed to prevent the overcollection and misuse of identity data. Governments, corporations, and third-party service providers often implement IAM solutions that track user behavior, location, and authentication history to enhance security. While identity monitoring is necessary for fraud detection and compliance, excessive data retention and invasive tracking practices can violate user privacy rights. Ethical IAM governance mandates that organizations implement clear data retention policies, anonymize logs where possible, and give users the ability to opt out of unnecessary tracking while maintaining secure authentication.

Transparency and accountability are foundational principles of ethical IAM governance. Users and organizations must have visibility into how identity data is processed, who has access to it, and under what conditions it can be shared. Implementing transparent IAM policies ensures that users understand consent mechanisms, access control policies, and identity verification requirements. Organizations must provide clear audit logs and real-time access reports that allow users to track authentication attempts, authorization decisions, and privilege escalations. Ethical IAM governance also requires establishing mechanisms for users to dispute access decisions, correct inaccurate identity data, and request the removal of outdated or unnecessary identity records.

Regulatory compliance serves as a framework for ethical IAM practices, ensuring that identity governance aligns with legal standards for data protection and privacy. Regulations such as the General Data Protection Regulation (GDPR), the California Consumer Privacy Act (CCPA), and the Digital Identity Frameworks in financial services mandate strict identity security and data governance requirements. Ethical IAM architectures must integrate privacy-by-design principles, enforce consent management, and ensure compliance with evolving regulatory mandates. By embedding ethical considerations into IAM governance, organizations can proactively address legal risks while fostering trust with users.

IAM accountability extends to how identity systems handle identity fraud, unauthorized access, and security breaches. Organizations must implement identity governance frameworks that detect and respond to credential misuse while ensuring that individuals are not falsely accused of fraud. Ethical IAM requires a balance between security enforcement and user rights, preventing excessive account lockouts, punitive access restrictions, and algorithmic decisions that unfairly penalize legitimate users. Identity governance tools must incorporate human oversight, allowing security teams to review and override automated access decisions when necessary.

Inclusive identity management is another key aspect of ethical IAM governance, ensuring that identity systems accommodate users from diverse backgrounds, technical literacy levels, and accessibility needs. Many IAM solutions rely on smartphone-based authentication, biometric verification, or internet-dependent identity checks, which may exclude users in regions with limited technological access. Ethical IAM architectures must support multiple authentication methods, including offline verification, government-issued identity credentials, and non-biometric authentication alternatives. Ensuring that identity systems are accessible to individuals with disabilities, non-traditional identity documentation, and varied language preferences is essential for equitable digital inclusion.

Decentralized identity frameworks enhance IAM ethics by reducing reliance on centralized identity providers and eliminating single points of control over user identities. Traditional IAM models place trust in a central authority, such as a government agency, corporate identity provider, or cloud IAM platform, creating risks of identity censorship, data monopolization, and external influence over authentication decisions. Decentralized Identity (DID) and Verifiable Credentials (VC) provide users with control over their identity attributes, enabling trust without dependence on a central entity. Ethical IAM governance must consider the benefits and risks of decentralized models, ensuring that they remain interoperable, secure, and resistant to fraud.

IAM security practices must also incorporate ethical decision-making frameworks to address the potential for identity misuse in sensitive contexts. Identity verification in law enforcement, border security, and public sector services must be designed to prevent discrimination, unauthorized surveillance, and wrongful identity profiling. Ethical IAM governance requires organizations to establish clear guidelines on identity data usage, implement oversight mechanisms, and prevent

IAM solutions from being used for unlawful or unethical purposes. Organizations deploying IAM in high-risk environments must establish ethics review boards and independent audits to ensure that identity systems uphold fundamental human rights.

User consent and identity data ownership must be central to ethical IAM governance. Many organizations collect and retain identity data without explicit user consent, leading to opaque data-sharing practices and potential privacy violations. Ethical IAM solutions must enforce consent-driven identity verification, where users have full visibility into how their identity data is shared, processed, and stored. Implementing dynamic consent mechanisms, such as granular user preferences for data-sharing permissions, ensures that individuals retain control over their digital identities. Organizations must also provide user-friendly interfaces for managing identity settings, revoking access, and requesting data deletion.

Future ethical considerations in IAM will focus on the intersection of artificial intelligence, blockchain-based identity verification, and biometric security. AI-driven identity systems must incorporate fairness metrics, explainability models, and continuous bias mitigation strategies to prevent discriminatory identity outcomes. Blockchain-based IAM solutions must address governance challenges related to immutable identity records and decentralized trust models. Biometric authentication systems must implement liveness detection, privacy-preserving encryption, and opt-in policies to ensure ethical use of facial recognition, fingerprint scanning, and voice authentication technologies.

Architecting IAM with ethical and accountable governance principles ensures that identity security remains aligned with human rights, regulatory compliance, and digital trust. By implementing transparent identity policies, minimizing data collection, reducing bias in AI-driven authentication, and enhancing user autonomy, organizations can build IAM solutions that prioritize security without compromising ethical standards. As digital identity ecosystems evolve, ethical IAM governance will play a critical role in shaping the future of identity security, ensuring that authentication and access management uphold fairness, privacy, and accountability in an increasingly interconnected world.

IAM in the Age of Super Apps: Architecting Identity for Unified Digital Ecosystems

Super apps have emerged as dominant platforms in digital ecosystems, consolidating multiple services into a single application that provides seamless access to financial services, e-commerce, ride-hailing, social networking, and entertainment. Unlike traditional applications that operate in isolated silos, super apps integrate diverse functionalities within a unified interface, creating complex identity management challenges. Identity and Access Management (IAM) must evolve to support these highly interconnected ecosystems, ensuring secure authentication, cross-service authorization, user privacy, and regulatory compliance. Architecting IAM for super apps requires balancing frictionless user experiences with robust security measures, managing multi-service identity federation, and enforcing adaptive authentication policies across a dynamic and expansive digital environment.

Super apps often operate as a platform of platforms, allowing third-party services to integrate within a shared identity framework. This creates a need for federated identity management that enables users to authenticate once and seamlessly access multiple services without repeated logins. Single Sign-On (SSO) solutions leveraging OpenID Connect (OIDC) and OAuth2 provide a foundation for seamless authentication, allowing users to maintain a consistent digital identity across all integrated services. Federated IAM models must enforce strong trust mechanisms, ensuring that third-party providers adhere to identity security policies while preventing unauthorized access to sensitive user data.

Authentication within super apps must support multiple identity verification methods, catering to diverse user bases across regions and services. Traditional username-password authentication is insufficient due to security risks and user experience limitations. Instead, Multi-Factor Authentication (MFA), passwordless authentication, and biometric verification must be integrated into IAM frameworks. Adaptive authentication further enhances security by assessing contextual risk factors, such as device reputation, geolocation, and behavioral biometrics, dynamically adjusting authentication requirements based on detected threats. Implementing step-up authentication ensures that high-risk transactions, such as financial payments or account modifications, require additional verification before execution.

Managing user identities in super apps requires a centralized identity store capable of handling millions of user records while ensuring privacy and security. Identity orchestration platforms enable seamless identity synchronization across multiple services, ensuring that profile updates, role changes, and access revocations are reflected consistently across the entire super app ecosystem. Privacy-enhancing IAM architectures must enforce data minimization principles, limiting the amount of personal information shared between services based on user consent. Decentralized identity models, such as Self-Sovereign Identity (SSI), provide users with greater control over their digital identities, enabling selective attribute disclosure without exposing unnecessary personal data.

Authorization in super apps must accommodate fine-grained access control policies that govern user permissions across multiple services. Traditional Role-Based Access Control (RBAC) models are often insufficient due to the dynamic nature of super apps, where users frequently transition between roles as consumers, merchants, and service providers. Attribute-Based Access Control (ABAC) enhances authorization by evaluating user attributes, contextual data, and transactional risk before granting access. Policy-Based Access Control (PBAC) further refines authorization decisions, enforcing business rules that adapt to changing security conditions and regulatory requirements.

Privileged Access Management (PAM) is essential for securing administrative functions within super apps, preventing unauthorized access to platform controls, financial transactions, and user data management interfaces. Just-In-Time (JIT) privilege escalation minimizes standing privileges by granting temporary administrative access only when necessary, reducing the risk of insider threats and credential abuse. Strong audit logging and session monitoring ensure that privileged access is continuously tracked, enabling rapid detection and response to suspicious activity.

IAM in super apps must integrate with fraud detection and risk analytics to prevent identity-based threats, including account takeovers, synthetic identity fraud, and credential stuffing attacks. User and Entity Behavior Analytics (UEBA) enhances security by monitoring login patterns, transaction behaviors, and privilege escalations for anomalies. If an IAM system detects unusual activity, such as multiple failed login attempts from different locations or unauthorized changes to payment settings, it can trigger automated security responses, including forced re-authentication, account locking, or risk-based transaction approval.

Data privacy compliance is a critical aspect of IAM in super apps, as these platforms collect, process, and share vast amounts of user information across multiple services. Regulations such as GDPR, CCPA, and emerging digital identity laws mandate strict data protection controls, requiring IAM solutions to enforce user consent management, data anonymization, and access transparency. Super apps must provide users with clear visibility into how their identity data is used, allowing them to manage consent settings, revoke permissions, and request data deletion. Implementing identity governance frameworks ensures that data access policies align with regulatory mandates, preventing unauthorized data sharing between integrated services.

IAM scalability is a fundamental requirement for super apps, as these platforms serve millions of users and process high volumes of authentication requests simultaneously. IAM architectures must leverage distributed identity services, load-balanced authentication endpoints, and caching mechanisms to ensure high availability and low-latency user authentication. Cloud-native IAM platforms, such as AWS Cognito, Azure AD B2C, and Google Cloud Identity, provide scalable identity management solutions capable of handling dynamic user growth while maintaining security and compliance. Edge-based authentication proxies and content delivery network (CDN) acceleration further enhance performance, optimizing authentication speeds for geographically dispersed user populations.

Super apps often incorporate decentralized and blockchain-based identity solutions to improve security, reduce reliance on centralized identity providers, and enhance user control over authentication data. Decentralized Identifiers (DIDs) and Verifiable Credentials (VCs) allow users to authenticate without storing sensitive identity attributes on a central server, reducing the risk of data breaches and identity theft. Blockchain-based IAM solutions also support tamper-proof identity verification, ensuring that identity claims, such as proof of age, financial history, or employment status, can be cryptographically validated without exposing raw personal data.

Future IAM developments in super apps will focus on AI-driven identity automation, biometric advancements, and seamless cross-border identity verification. AI-powered IAM solutions will enhance adaptive authentication by continuously learning from user behavior and dynamically adjusting identity policies in real time. Advancements in biometric security, including liveness detection and multimodal authentication, will strengthen identity verification, reducing the risk of biometric spoofing attacks. Global identity federation standards will enable super apps to support cross-border authentication, allowing users to verify identities across international digital ecosystems without redundant identity registration.

By architecting IAM solutions that support seamless authentication, fine-grained authorization, regulatory compliance, and fraud prevention, super apps can deliver secure and user-friendly digital experiences. Implementing federated identity management, adaptive security controls, and scalable IAM infrastructures ensures that these platforms remain resilient against evolving identity threats while maintaining trust in unified digital ecosystems. As super apps continue to expand, IAM strategies must evolve to support their complex identity requirements, providing secure, scalable, and privacy-centric identity management solutions for the next generation of digital platforms.

IAM Leadership and Strategy: Transitioning from IAM Engineer to IAM Architect

Identity and Access Management (IAM) is a dynamic field that requires both technical expertise and strategic vision. While IAM engineers focus on implementing authentication mechanisms, access controls, and identity federation, IAM architects take on a broader role, designing scalable, resilient, and policy-driven identity frameworks for the enterprise. Transitioning from an IAM engineer to an IAM architect requires a shift in mindset from hands-on technical execution to high-level strategy, governance, and long-term planning. This evolution involves mastering IAM architecture principles, understanding business objectives, influencing organizational security strategies, and aligning IAM initiatives with regulatory compliance and risk management frameworks.

The first step in moving from an IAM engineer to an IAM architect is developing a deep understanding of IAM architectural frameworks, industry best practices, and emerging identity trends. Engineers are typically responsible for configuring identity providers (IdPs), integrating IAM solutions with enterprise applications, and managing authentication and authorization flows. However, architects must design identity ecosystems that support the organization's long-term scalability, security posture, and regulatory requirements. This requires expertise in IAM design principles, including Zero Trust security, adaptive authentication, decentralized identity, and cloud-native identity architectures.

An IAM architect must move beyond the tactical aspects of IAM deployment and focus on strategic identity governance. Identity Governance and Administration (IGA) is a critical area where architects must define policies for identity lifecycle management, role-based access control (RBAC), attribute-based access control (ABAC), and privileged access management (PAM). Governance frameworks, such as NIST 800-63, ISO 27001, and CIS IAM benchmarks, provide guidelines for designing IAM strategies that balance security with operational efficiency. An IAM architect must be able to translate these guidelines into actionable policies that ensure compliance while enabling business agility.

Communication and leadership skills are essential for an IAM architect, as they must collaborate with cross-functional teams, security executives, and business stakeholders to drive IAM initiatives. Unlike engineers, who primarily interact with technical teams, architects engage with C-level executives, compliance officers, product managers, and risk management teams to align IAM strategies with broader enterprise goals. The ability to present IAM roadmaps, justify security investments, and advocate for IAM best practices is crucial for influencing decision-making at the organizational level.

IAM architects must also develop expertise in enterprise IAM integration, ensuring that identity solutions seamlessly connect with cloud platforms, SaaS applications, and legacy on-premises systems. Engineers typically focus on implementing identity federation using protocols such as SAML, OAuth2, and OpenID Connect. However, architects must design identity architectures that support multi-cloud and hybrid environments, enabling secure authentication across AWS, Azure, Google Cloud, and third-party SaaS applications. This requires an understanding of IAM automation, identity orchestration, and cross-domain identity federation strategies.

Security risk management is another critical area for IAM architects. Engineers focus on implementing security controls, such as Multi-Factor Authentication (MFA) and role-based access policies, while architects must assess IAM risks from a broader organizational perspective. This includes evaluating insider threat risks, identity-related attack vectors, third-party access vulnerabilities, and compliance risks. Architects must work closely with security operations teams to implement User and Entity Behavior Analytics (UEBA), identity threat detection, and automated risk-based authentication to mitigate identity-related security threats.

IAM architects must also have a strong grasp of regulatory compliance and legal frameworks that impact identity security. Unlike engineers, who focus on technical IAM configurations, architects must ensure that IAM solutions comply with regulations such as GDPR, HIPAA, PCI-DSS, SOX, and emerging digital identity laws. This involves defining access control policies, implementing identity audit mechanisms, and ensuring that identity governance frameworks align with regulatory requirements. Understanding how IAM policies affect data protection, privacy laws, and access management ensures that organizations avoid compliance violations and security breaches.

Architects must also be proficient in IAM automation and Infrastructure as Code (IaC) to support scalable identity deployments. Engineers may focus on configuring IAM solutions manually, but architects design automated identity provisioning, role assignment, and access certification workflows using tools such as Terraform, AWS CloudFormation, and Ansible. By automating IAM processes, architects reduce administrative overhead, enhance security consistency, and enable self-service identity management for employees, partners, and customers.

A successful IAM architect must also stay ahead of industry trends and emerging identity technologies. Engineers often focus on maintaining and optimizing existing IAM solutions, while architects explore next-generation IAM innovations, such as Self-Sovereign Identity (SSI), Decentralized Identifiers (DIDs), verifiable credentials, and blockchain-based identity verification. Keeping up with advancements in AI-driven identity analytics, passwordless authentication, and Zero Trust IAM frameworks ensures that architects design future-proof identity ecosystems that can adapt to evolving security threats and business requirements.

IAM architects play a key role in IAM strategy and investment planning, ensuring that identity solutions align with business objectives while optimizing costs. Engineers may focus on deploying IAM tools, but architects must evaluate IAM platforms, compare licensing models, and assess the total cost of ownership (TCO) of identity security solutions. This includes determining whether cloud-based Identity as a Service (IDaaS) models provide cost-effective alternatives to on-premises IAM deployments. Additionally, architects must justify IAM investments to executives by demonstrating return on investment (ROI), risk reduction, and operational efficiencies achieved through identity automation and security enhancements.

Developing soft skills, including negotiation, strategic thinking, and executive communication, is essential for engineers transitioning to IAM architects. Engineers are accustomed to solving technical challenges, but architects must navigate complex business dynamics, manage IAM roadmaps, and build consensus among diverse stakeholders. This requires the ability to translate technical IAM concepts into business language, explaining how identity security impacts revenue, customer experience, and regulatory compliance.

To transition from an IAM engineer to an IAM architect, professionals should seek opportunities to lead IAM projects, contribute to security strategy discussions, and engage in IAM governance planning. Gaining experience in designing IAM frameworks, evaluating IAM vendor solutions, and participating in security architecture reviews helps build the skills needed for architectural leadership. Certifications such as Certified Information Systems Security Professional (CISSP), Certified Information Security Manager (CISM), and specialized IAM credentials like Certified Identity and Access Manager (CIAM) can further validate expertise in IAM architecture and strategy.

Becoming an IAM architect requires a shift from hands-on implementation to strategic IAM leadership. By mastering IAM governance, regulatory compliance, risk management, and identity architecture, engineers can advance into IAM architect roles, shaping the future of enterprise identity security and driving digital transformation through secure, scalable, and intelligent IAM solutions.

www.ingramcontent.com/pod-product-compliance
Lightning Source LLC
LaVergne TN
LVHW051230050326
832903LV00028B/2331